_IMPROVE YOUR HEART HEALTH
_BOOST YOUR BRAIN POWER
_DECREASE STRESS HORMONES
AND CHRONIC FATIGUE
_75 DELICIOUS RECIPES

Superfoods for life

CACAO

Matt Ruscigno M.P.H., R.D. with *Joshua Ploeg*

D1220691

Fair Winds Press
100 Cummings Center, Suite 406L
Beverly, MA 01915

fairwindspress.com • quarryspoon.com

FAIR WINDS

© 2014 Fair Winds Press

First published in the USA in 2014 by
Fair Winds Press, a member of
Quarto Publishing Group USA Inc.
100 Cummings Center, Suite 406-L
Beverly, MA 01915-6101
www.fairwindspress.com

Visit www.QuarrySPOON.com and help us celebrate food and culture one
spoonful at a time!

18 17 16 15 14   1 2 3 4 5

ISBN: 978-1-59233-610-4

Digital edition published in 2014

eISBN: 978-1-62788-026-8

Library of Congress Cataloging-in-Publication Data available

Cover design by Paul Burgess
Book design by Kathie Alexander
Book layout by Laura H. Couallier, Laura Herrmann Design
Photography by Glenn Scott Photography

Printed and bound in China

*The information in this book is for educational purposes only. It is not
intended to replace the advice of a physician or medical practitioner. Please
see your health care provider before beginning any new health program.*

Dedication

Dedicated to everyone working
to make our food system more
just and more delicious.

From the workers to the activists,
from the researchers to the chefs:
you keep me motived.

*10% of author royalties will be donated
to the Food Empowerment Project.*

CONTENTS

Cacao

Cacao: An Introduction to This Delicious Nutritional Powerhouse

The cacao bean, from which chocolate is made, is known as a superfood for its many nutritional benefits. It has an incredibly rich history of varied uses from drinks to coins to rituals, but today in the Western world, it has, unfortunately, become mostly just a candy bar.

Yet it has so much more to offer. From mousse (page 138) to lasagna (page 82) to huitlacoche-chocolate empanadas (page 133), the phenomenal cacao bean can make its way into your diet in so many ways. And not only will your taste buds thank you, but your brain and heart will, too.

Cacao isn't your run-of-the-mill healthy food; it's a superstar among superfoods. We have heard quite a lot about the phytochemical content of tea, wine, and blueberries. But cacao has more than all of them. And though these foods are great, you can consume them in only so many ways. How many dishes can you make with tea or wine? There are probably more culinary uses of cacao than there are ways to eat blueberries! We are talking about a nutrient-dense, phytochemical-rich food that can be eaten in breakfasts, desserts, and every way in between.

You don't need to be a super-adventurous eater or fringe chef to use cacao in new ways and reap the benefits of this superbean. We've developed not just a few, but seventy-five one-of-a-kind recipes to get cacao into your nutrition plan in an easy and delicious way.

What Makes Cacao a Superfood?

- **Cacao has an insanely high phytochemical and antioxidant content.** These naturally occurring chemical compounds are the future of nutrition, disease prevention, and good health. Cacao is loaded with them. You'll learn more about this in chapter 2.

- **It's nutrient dense.** Cacao is full of minerals, fiber, and healthy dietary fat. These nutrients in combination with the phytochemicals may help lower your risk of heart disease, stroke, and more. We discuss the research in chapters 3 and 4.

- **It makes you happy.** Chocolate may be the most craved food in the world. It's full of (good!) chemicals that affect our brain and our mood. We discuss this in chapter 5. How super is that?

- **It's a great accompaniment to physical activity.** In chapter 6, we discuss how soldiers, hikers, and others with serious physical demands have long used chocolate in times of great nutritional need. Today, it's popular in drinks and other workout foods during and after exercise because of its caloric density and antioxidant content.

- **Chocolate is a high-quality food with subtle tastes, like good coffee or wine.** In the appendix, we discuss the various types of chocolate available and their distinctions and classifications. Organic? Raw? Fair trade? We've got your preferences covered.

- **It's extremely versatile.** From Quinoa–Chocolate Chip Energy Bars (page 46) to Ghoulishly Delicious Goulash (page 100) and Flavanol-Full Chocolate Pudding (page 161) cacao can be added to any nutrition plan.

- **It's commonplace and accessible.** Most everyone is familiar with chocolate and enjoys the taste. Although some work may be required to find high-quality cacao and chocolate, it is available more readily than most people realize.

- **You only need to consume a small amount to get the benefits.** Most of the research on cacao is done using cocoa powder—a low-calorie, nutrient-dense powder that, as you'll learn in this book, can be added to a plethora of foods and dishes.

Milk Chocolate Is Not the Healthiest Way to Get Your Cacao

Milk chocolate, the most commonly eaten chocolate in the United States, contains very little cacao, often less than 10 percent. Instead, the majority of what you are eating are added sweeteners, dairy products, and other less healthful, refined ingredients.

The health benefits we've discussed in this book are specific to cacao; therefore, milk chocolate may not be the best way to get the benefits. It's important to read the label and to know how much cacao and other added ingredients are in what you are eating. If you are used to milk chocolate, start with the highest cacao percentage you enjoy and work your way toward darker, higher-cacao chocolate. If the cacao percentage is not offered on the label, see how high up and how often it is mentioned in the ingredients. Ideally, there is more cacao per weight than sugar or dairy products, and it will therefore appear higher on the ingredient label.

Additionally, milk may contain GMOs in the form of recombinant bovine growth hormone (rBGH). This is a genetically engineered variation on a naturally occurring hormone injected into dairy cows to increase milk production. It is banned for human consumption in the European Union, Canada, New Zealand, and Australia. Non-GMO certified and organic milks and milk chocolates do not contain rBGH.

Cacao: A Long and Intriguing History

Today, we are fortunate to have some pretty amazing and unique research on cacao. We know it has properties that are good for our hearts, it may protect our skin from harmful UV rays, and its smell alone may increase the number of books people buy at bookstores. Seriously, a group of Belgian researchers found that customers who could smell chocolate were 40 percent more likely to purchase a cookbook or romance novel and about 22 percent more likely to buy other books. Chocolate is one of those foods that we love to hear good things about because who doesn't love it?

People have loved chocolate, or at least cacao, the main ingredient in chocolate, for a very long time. The history of cacao goes back hundreds of years to pre-Columbian Mesoamerica, where the earliest proof of cacao consumption exists. The Mayans cultivated cacao as early as 300 CE on the Yucatan Peninsula. The Aztecs, 1,200 years later, were still using it regularly for a drink called *xocolatl*. Meaning "bitter water," xocolatl was a cold, savory drink made with chiles, cloves, cinnamon, and cornmeal. The cornmeal acted as an emulsifier of sorts between the water and the fatty content of the cacao bean. It was very different from what most people imagine as a chocolate drink. Legend has it that Montezuma II drank fifty cups a day! No doubt he felt a prolonged rush from consuming large quantities of theobromine, a bitter, mildly stimulant alkaloid, and caffeine.

And we'd be remiss to mention the history and benefits of cacao and not discuss the Kuna Indians who live on the San Blas Islands off the coast of Panama. They drink huge quantities of cacao to this day and have the health benefits to prove the super-ness of this superfood. Deaths from cancer, hypertension, and cardio-vascular disease are extremely rare in this group of people. Why? Consumption of cacao drinks, estimated at 30 to 40 ounces (0.9 to 1.2 L) a day, is a part of their everyday life on the islands—which isn't too far from where the first traces of cacao consumption were found.

Kuna who move to mainland Panama and adopt the eating habits of other Panamanians lose the health benefits. Their blood pressure goes up, and hypertension becomes commonplace. Their rate of chronic disease soon mirrors the mainlanders. And the research suggests this is because they have stopped drinking cacao in large amounts. In other words, they gave up a traditional diet that included cacao to a more Westernized, urban diet rife with nutrition-related diseases.

Cacao itself went through a Westernization process when it was brought to Europe 400 years ago. At first it remained a savory drink, but within a hundred years, sugar became a regular ingredient. For a long while it was a drink of only the rich and elite of society. That changed around the time of the Industrial Revolution with the help of the Quakers. Well known for their promotion of justice and equality, the Quakers, who also invented an early version of the Monopoly game, brought chocolate to the masses. They saw it as a nourishing, healthy drink that was an alternative to alcohol. The Quakers settled in Pennsylvania, where names associated with chocolate to this day, such as Cadbury and Hershey, got their start in the chocolate business. Once the milk chocolate bar was invented, cacao became a less prominent ingredient, and its association with health all but disappeared.

Achieving the Health Benefits of the Kuna Indians with Cacao

We may not want 40 ounces (1.2 L) of the Kunas' cacao drink every day, but we can probably add some cacao to our diet pretty easily. In the United States, most people still love their chocolate sweetened with sugar and added milk, but it doesn't have to be this way. We can use the cacao bean before much is added and focus on the beneficial properties—and enjoy it in a new way. People often say, "How can chocolate be a health food?" and my response is simply, "Minimize all of the unhealthy ingredients!"

Currently there is a resurgence of "medicinal" cacao along with a much wider scope of use than simply as a confectionary. Similar to their consumption of coffee, people today have grown accustomed to the subtle yet complex taste of cacao and are enjoying it now almost like it was 500 years ago. Artisanal, small batches of single-source chocolate aren't quite commonplace (yet!) but are available now more than ever.

Cacao: From Humble Beginnings to Nearly Invisible

Chances are you have never seen a cacao bean. Most people, unless they are involved in some level of chocolate production, have never seen one. Cacao beans are not easy to find. I was chatting with a chocolate aficionado and mentioned that my local cooperative grocery store carries them, and she admitted to having never actually seen one. This bean is where chocolate-anything begins. And from here, we develop a number of different products, all with unique tastes, uses, and nutritional properties. Let's take a look at them all, starting with the whole cacao bean.

- **Cacao beans.** The cacao bean is the dried fatty seed of the fruit of the cocoa tree, *Theobroma cacao*. After the drying process, it is often fermented and/or roasted. It is rare, but possible, to find whole cacao beans available for sale, raw or roasted. They are very popular among raw foodists and are eaten directly as snacks or added to smoothies and raw dishes. They have a bitter taste, and if you are expecting chocolate, you are in for a surprise! The benefits of using the whole bean are that you are in control of the whole food. You know exactly what you are getting.

- **Cacao nibs.** Cacao nibs are cracked, shelled cacao beans. They are usually roasted but can be found in their raw state. They are sold at health food stores and specialty shops and are available online. They are considered a whole food and therefore contain a high level of beneficial antioxidants, fiber, and other nutrients. They also are on the bitter side, like cacao beans.

Because none of the cocoa butter has been removed, they are also high in fat. Using nibs in cooking is beneficial because they are easier to find and they are already shelled and broken into smaller pieces.

- **Cacao powder, raw or roasted.** Not to be confused with cocoa powder, cacao powder is made from grinding down the shelled cacao bean. It can be either raw or roasted depending on the treatment of the original cacao beans. It contains the fatty components of the bean and is therefore high in fat, unlike cocoa powder. The texture is also much different because the fat gives it a much richer look and feel. Cacao powder is beneficial because the powder form is extremely versatile—you will find a number of recipes in this book that use it. It can be added to smoothies and other simple foods with ease.

- **Cocoa liquor.** Cocoa liquor is the paste made from ground, roasted, shelled, and fermented cocoa beans. It contains both nonfat cocoa solids, commonly just called cocoa powder, and cocoa butter. Cocoa liquor is what is referred to as "percent cacao" on food packaging. It is pure chocolate in fluid form!

- **Cocoa butter.** When cocoa liquor is pressed and the cocoa solids are re-moved, slightly more than half of the remaining product is the cacao fat, cocoa butter. It is 100 percent fat and has many uses in food and cosmetics. During the production of chocolate bars, it is added back to the cocoa liquor.

- **Cocoa powder.** Cocoa powder is what is left after the cocoa butter has been removed from the liquor. It is one of the most recognized forms of cacao and is what is most commonly used in research. Because the cocoa butter has been removed, it is much lower in fat and is often referred to as non-fat cocoa solids. Despite seeming to be a refined food, it retains much of the micronutrients found in the cacao bean, such as zinc, calcium, copper, magnesium, and potassium. It is also still high in flavonoids, the beneficial phytochemicals that cacao is known for. It is one of the most common forms of cacao and is widely available.

- **Chocolate bars.** Chocolate bars are a solid food made by combining cocoa liquor with cocoa butter and (usually) sugar and/or milk. The proportion of cocoa liquor in the final product determines how dark the chocolate is. From a nutritional standpoint, the darker a chocolate is, the better because it contains a higher percentage of cacao. What's one of the obvious benefits of chocolate bars? They are delicious.

- **Baking chocolate.** Baking chocolate, also known as semisweet or bittersweet chocolate, is a dark chocolate and must be no less than 35 percent cocoa liquor. It is often very dark because unsweetened versions contain no sugar or other added ingredients.

- **Milk chocolate.** Milk chocolate is made by adding condensed or powdered milk to the chocolate mixture. The type of chocolate consumed most in the United States is milk chocolate, which typically contains only 10 to 12 percent cocoa liquor. When discussing the health benefits of cacao, it's important to make the distinction between milk chocolate bars, which have very little cacao, and the other products listed previously, which contain much larger percentages of the bean.

- **White chocolate.** White chocolate contains only cocoa butter (at least 20 percent by weight) combined with sweeteners and (usually) dairy ingredients. It does not contain any cocoa and therefore has none of the associated benefits. In many scientific studies looking at the benefits of cacao, the control group is given white chocolate because it does not have the beneficial phytochemicals.

Why Plant-Based Cacao Recipes?

It is no coincidence that every superfood comes from plants. In today's world, we have become far removed from our food, and what most people eat bears little resemblance to the plant or animal it started as. But throughout human history, we have used a large variety of plants for our sustenance. We eat the fruit of plants with ease and recognize it as such. We think less about the seeds, stems, roots, leaves, and flowers that make up a significant percentage of the world's food. Plant foods are nutritionally dense, which means they have lots of nutrients for very few calories; hence the old adage recommending you eat your fruits and vegetables.

Keeping with the spirit of eating more plants and more superfoods, the recipes in this book are plant based and vegan. There's a lot to gain by learning more about cacao and plant-based nutrition as well as making some of these delicious cacao recipes part of your nutrition plan.

What Does "Plant-Based" Mean?

"Plant-based" has become a popular phrase recently, though it is not precisely defined. Some use it as a synonym for veganism, which is a diet that avoids all animal products. Others believe that plant-based does not included any refined, processed foods (which are also poorly defined!). It is most commonly used to mean "flexitarianism," in which one eats mostly, but not strictly, vegetarian. My personal definition of plant-based is a diet pattern of predominantly whole plant foods including whole grains, vegetables, legumes, fruits, nuts, and seeds.

The nutritional benefits of plant-based eating include the following:

1. More phytochemicals and antioxidants
2. Healthy, unsaturated fats
3. Increased fiber
4. Synergistic benefit of whole foods
5. More volume, fewer calories

RECIPE INTRODUCTION from Joshua Ploeg

When the Spanish first arrived in the Americas and were introduced to chocolate, it was a far cry from what most chocolate consumers are accustomed to today. It was crushed up without any sweetener and mottled with spices, sometimes cornmeal and seeds, chiles, and water into a froth and drunk—sometimes hot, sometimes cold. The Spanish found it bitter, wild, and intense and were a bit aghast at how obsessively Montezuma and his court seemed to drink it. They just didn't understand it but nonetheless thought it might have a use when brought back to Europe.

Europeans were a bit hostile to the taste of cacao, so it was not long before sweeteners were added to take the edge off. (At first, though, even some Europeans found it a treat with cinnamon and vanilla.) It took a little while for sweetened versions to take over, but once that happened, the popularity of cocoa exploded, and the Europeans claimed it as one of their own. And look where we are with chocolate today: cookies, cakes, pies, candy bars, hot cocoa, and chocolatinis to satisfy your sweet tooth and make you feel good (notice the difference between feeling good and feeling go-o-o-o-d; the second is all about consuming more and more, rather than being satisfied, which is interesting considering that chocolate *should* help you feel satiated).

You will immediately notice that most of the recipes in this book are savory recipes. That is because we hope that you will begin to view chocolate a little differently—in a new way (or actually, a bit more of the *old* way!). Its continued pairing with a lot of sugar has caused most Americans and Europeans to no longer appreciate a good old piece of unsweetened chocolate or a sprinkling of unvarnished cacao powder. People think it is too bitter. Bitterness has been undervalued for a while in Western society, yet it is one of the five flavors, and many of us enjoy coffee, horseradish, citrus rinds, grapefruit, and Campari, so how averse to bitterness can we really be?

We just think of it as that first visceral reaction to the initial bitter taste rather than what potential the taste of bitterness has to bring out—to complement and to challenge the other tastes and flavors.

Think again.

That is more the fault of the overabundance of sweeteners in our society than the fault of the root ingredient. We ask you to reimagine your introduction to chocolate, to appreciate it as a base flavor with a good degree of depth and subtlety, and to think of it as first a nondessert ingredient. Like a number of things (coffee comes to mind) that were adopted through colonialism, cacao was morphed and twisted to the European palate and sensibility, so much so that you will find that the processed European methods of using and enjoying chocolate are considered to be "correct." Chocolate, even processed chocolate, serves a different aesthetic in Mexico if you have traveled there much. Fairly commonly you will find it mixed with spices, cornmeal, chiles, too sweet, not sweet at all, grainy, mixed with water, made into fabulous moles, and other such supposed no-nos according to European construction.

In a way, you may soon be inclined to "decolonize" your palate. To be fair, craft chocolate making has more recently come around to the less sweet, the daring flavor additions, and the higher cacao contents. That said, sugar, like many foods, can be fine in modest quantities, so we don't attempt to completely divest from it here. Rather, we try to use it a bit more judiciously (a few syrups excepted here and there). Nor does cooking and processing rob cacao of all of its beneficial properties. So we do not avoid that either.

Ease yourself into unsweetened chocolate and soon you may find it to be sweet enough for your liking. Bittersweet, dark, unsweetened, or high-cacao chocolates and powders are exclusively called for in this book, rather than milk chocolate or some of the more sugary bars.

Cacao in its many forms can add a subtle or strong earthiness, a rich body, a powerful grounding influence, or a heavenly elevation to a dish in concert with a surprisingly large number of complementary ingredients. From those born of earth such as sweet potatoes and mushrooms, to those rich and in the air such as avocados and coconut; from the spicy bravado of chiles, onions, and garlic to the cloying intrigue of cinnamon, coriander, vanilla, and turmeric; from the sweet and tangy realms of dates and tamarind to the acidic and sharp but nuanced hues of tomato and citrus, cacao brings out and complements seldom-noticed qualities of other foods and shades their more outrageous or familiar qualities. It works wonders in unexpected places and combines with old partners in new and innovative ways in the hands and mind of the creative individual—such as you!

Experiment, enjoy, live, and discover for yourself which combinations work for you. You will be thankful that you did, and we are grateful for the opportunity to assist you in discovering the depth and power of cacao and feeling comfortable incorporating it into your diet without guilt.

Yours in chocolate,

Chef Joshua Ploeg

How to Melt Chocolate

Many of the recipes in this book call for you to melt chocolate. Below is a list of ways you can do that. To start, coarsely chop chocolate bars or chunks into fairly equal-size pieces to ensure even melting.

- **Direct heat:** Place the chocolate in a heavy saucepan over very low heat and stir gently but constantly until the chocolate begins to melt. Times can vary, but it should take about 2 to 4 minutes. Immediately remove the pan from the heat and stir the chocolate until it is smooth.

- **Double boiler:** This method eliminates the possibility of scorching the chocolate and involves two pots, with one that sits partway in the other. Place water in the bottom pot so the top of the water is ½ inch (1 cm) below the upper pot. Place chocolate in the upper pot. Then place the double boiler over low heat. Stir the chocolate constantly until it is melted. The water in the bottom of the double boiler should not come to boiling while the chocolate is melting.

  To create a makeshift double boiler, use a medium-small pot for the bottom and a mixing bowl that fits snugly (and high) in the pot for the top.

- **Microwave oven:** Place up to 8 ounces (225 g) of chopped chocolate in a microwave-safe bowl, ramekin, or measuring cup. Microwave, uncovered, at 50 percent power for 1½ to 2 minutes or until the chocolate is soft enough to stir smooth. This might take a bit longer. You may also microwave it on high if you wish, but do this for very short time periods (such as 20- to 30-second intervals) and check after each blast to make sure the chocolate is not scorching. The chocolate will hold its shape after it starts to melt, so stir it once every minute during heating.

  Use dry utensils to prevent the chocolate from seizing (turning thick and lumpy). If adding liquid to melted chocolate, the liquid should be hot as well.

Putting It into Practice

At the end of each chapter, "Putting It into Practice" will offer practical tips and advice for making the most of what you have learned. Food is best experienced, not read about, and we want to make that transition as easy and healthy as possible for you. So with that in mind, consider these tips:

- **Eat chocolate slowly.** As noted previously in this chapter, the subtleties of chocolate take time to get used to, like a good wine or cup of coffee. As a friend of mine with a small-batch chocolate company says, "Fine chocolate is both undervalued and misunderstood."

- **Look for quality cacao products.** Search where you currently shop and consider shopping at new stores. Finding cacao products and high-quality chocolate requires a little extra time and work. Ask questions and don't be intimidated!

- **Become label savvy.** The nutrition label and ingredient lists are very useful tools in understanding what we are eating. Look for the percentage of cacao in your dark chocolate bars and the added ingredients, both good and bad. You want less sugar, regardless of what type of sugar is added.

- **Aim high.** Gradually increase the highest percentage of dark chocolate you are comfortable with. A number of these recipes will be new to you, so take time to adjust your palate to these unique food combinations and tastes.

- **Slow down.** Make time for healthy changes and for cooking with new ingredients. Cooking and eating is an adventure, rife with ups and downs. Enjoy it!

CHAPTER ONE

Recipes at a Glance

- Raw Chocolate-Carrot Cake 23
- Baby Carrots with Lemon and Chocolate 24
- Wow! Chocolate Dinner Enchiladas 27
- Aztec-Style Chocolate Drink (Two Ways) 28
- Surprisingly Succulent Baba Ghanoush 30
- Never-Fail Cocoamole 31
- Basic but Wholly Scrumptious Fudge 32
- Delicious, Judicious, and Nutritious Juice with Cacao 33
- Stunning Raw Cacao-Veggie Four-Layer Stack 34
- Raw Spaghetti Squash-Cacao Nests 35

A note on the recipes regarding flour, oil, gluten and other restrictions: There are many paths to good health and many ideas about the ideal foods to eat. We've created these recipes with balance in mind; they are healthy and plant-based, but designed to be accessible for most people. If you have spent a lot of time thinking about nutrition and live by a stricter set of standards than we have laid out here, we invite you to adjust the recipes as needed. If you avoid fractionated oil, gluten, or white flour, for instance, you can modify these recipes using the substitutes and variations to which you are accustomed.

Raw Chocolate-Carrot Cake

This is a very creative raw dish that combines the healthy fats found in raw cacao and cashews with the fat-soluble beta-carotene found in carrots. Raisins supply much of the sweetness, and coconut and banana make this healthy delight more dessert-like.

FOR THE CAKE:

½ cup (55 g) grated apple, with a little salt and lemon juice on it

1 cup (110 g) grated carrot

½ cup (43 g) dried coconut flakes

1 cup (140 g) chopped cashews

½ teaspoon sea salt

½ cup (75 g) golden raisins

2 to 3 tablespoons (40 to 60 g) agave nectar or other sweetener

½ cup (48 g) raw cacao powder

½ cup (113 g) mashed banana

1 teaspoon ground ginger

1 teaspoon ground cinnamon

¼ teaspoon ground cloves

FOR THE FROSTING:

½ cup (113 g) mashed banana

2 to 3 tablespoons (14 to 21 g) coconut powder

1 tablespoon (6 g) cacao powder

1 tablespoon (20 g) agave nectar or other sweetener (optional)

1 tablespoon (15 ml) lemon juice

¼ teaspoon salt

¼ teaspoon powdered mustard

TO MAKE THE CAKE: Grind all the cake ingredients in a food processor and divide among 8 ramekins (the serving size is a little more than ½ cup [115 g]). If you prefer bigger chunks of everything for a better personality, then leave the texture intact and mix by hand rather than grinding together in the food processor—it's your choice!

TO MAKE THE FROSTING: Blend all the frosting ingredients and adjust the seasonings to taste. Frost the cakes and chill before serving.

Yield: 8 servings

Baby Carrots with Lemon and Chocolate

This is an easy way to spruce up some boring old baby carrots. Actually, even just grating chocolate on plain cooked carrots will spruce them up. Carrots are well known for their beta-carotene content (the name even comes from carrots!), but did you know they may reduce your risk of coronary heart disease? A study out of the Netherlands looking at the diet of more than 20,000 people found that those who consumed carrots regularly reduced their risk by 32 percent! Combined with cacao, they make a heart-healthy super side.

2 cups (260 g) baby carrots

1 minced or pressed garlic clove

¼ cup (40 g) diced white onion

1 tablespoon (15 ml) olive oil

½ teaspoon salt, or to taste

¼ teaspoon black pepper

6 lemon slices, about ¼ inch (6 mm) thick

2 teaspoons minced fresh oregano

¼ cup (60 ml) vegetable broth

2 ounces (55 g) bittersweet chocolate, chopped

1 tablespoon (16 g) tomato paste

Sauté the carrots, garlic, and onion in the olive oil in a medium-size saucepan over medium heat with some of the salt and pepper for 3 minutes. Add the lemon, oregano, and broth and cook for 5 minutes more. Stir in the chocolate and tomato paste and cook for an additional 2 to 3 minutes. Add additional salt and pepper to taste. Serve warm.

Yield: 4 servings

Wow! Chocolate Dinner Enchiladas

The ever-popular enchilada is even more enticing with the addition of chocolate! Part of the fun here is taking something you love and improving the healthiness and taste at the same time. Depending on what you use to fill it, this can be quite an exciting and healthful dish. Vegetables and vegetable-based fats replace the saturated animal fats from the cheese and meat that are often found in enchiladas. Tortillas other than corn may also be used for this, of course!

12 to 14 corn tortillas

2 cups (475 ml) water
(or enough to cover the tortillas)

¼ cup (60 ml) lime juice

3 to 4 cups (750 g to 1 kg) One-Hour Mole
(page 50) or enchilada sauce (page 113),
divided

1 cup (150 g) crumbled firm tofu

1 cup (30 g) chopped spinach

½ cup (80 g) diced onion

¼ cup (35 g) cornmeal

½ teaspoon chili powder

2 minced garlic cloves

½ teaspoon salt (or to taste)

1 tablespoon (15 ml) olive oil

1 teaspoon dried crushed oregano

2 teaspoons cider vinegar

¼ cup (24 g) raw cacao powder

¼ cup (4 g) chopped fresh cilantro

¼ teaspoon black pepper

½ cup (50 g) chopped toasted almonds,
(68 g) pine nuts, or other fun nut

Preheat the oven to 375°F (190°C, gas mark 5).

In a large, shallow bowl or baking dish, soak the tortillas in the water and lime juice for 2 to 3 minutes. Drain and shake the tortillas before using (this makes them less likely to crack). Return to the bowl or dish and spread them out a little, though it's okay if they overlap.

Spoon ½ cup (125 g) of the sauce into the bottom of a greased 9- × 13-inch (23 × 33 cm) baking or casserole dish. Mix together the tofu through the nuts and season to taste. Divide evenly among the tortillas, roll each one up, and place in the dish on top of the sauce. Pour the rest of the sauce over the top. Bake for 40 minutes.

VARIATIONS: Instead of the tofu, try using 1 cup (70 g) mushrooms, (99 g) cooked eggplant, (205 g) squash, (136 g) sweet potato, (225 g) potato, or try a combo!

Yield: 6 servings

Aztec-Style Chocolate Drink (Two Ways)

This drink is based on the original Aztec cacao beverage, where they ground the beans into a mealy powder and cooked it with water and spices. Some drank it obsessively back in the day, and if anything can get you excited about unsweetened chocolate, this can. Think of it like coffee, chicory, or maté. I also included the cold beverage version as well for your experimental pleasure.

½ cup (48 g) raw cacao powder or (112 g) nibs

3 cups (700 ml) water

1 teaspoon fresh or dried minced chile pepper, or to taste

1 cinnamon stick, crushed

Pinch salt

1 vanilla bean

With a mortar and pestle, grind the nibs into a powder, or if your powder has pieces in it, grind that to a finer texture. You can also use a food processor.

Add the water, chile, and cinnamon stick to a medium-size pot, bring to a boil, reduce the heat, and simmer for 10 minutes. Drain, saving the chile water. Mix the chile water with the cacao, cinnamon stick, and salt. Bring to a boil, stirring. Lower to simmer and cook for 15 to 20 minutes. Scrape the vanilla bean and add both the scrapings and the bean to the concoction for the last few minutes of simmering. Serve hot or warm.

Yield: 4 servings or 1 big one if you're Montezuma

And Here's the Uncooked Version!

½ cup (48 g) raw cacao powder or (112 g) nibs

¼ cup (35 g) cornmeal

¼ cup (35 g) squash seeds

Pinch salt

1 dried chile pepper, crushed and seeded

2 cups (475 ml) water

In a sturdy medium mixing bowl, grind all of the ingredients except the water with a pestle. Continue grinding while adding the water slowly until a thick but drinkable consistency is reached, about 4 to 5 minutes. (You may not have to use all of the water to get this to your satisfaction.)

Next, whip the mixture with a whisk until a bit frothy, which will only take a few minutes. Serve.

NOTE: You can also serve this beverage heated. This will make for a slightly smaller amount than the hot chocolate recipe, but you can still put it in 4 mugs.

Yield: 4 servings

Surprisingly Succulent Baba Ghanoush

The chocolate really brings this recipe to life! This will make your gears turn, imagining the different ways you could use chocolate and eggplant together. Eggplant is very low in calories yet high in fiber and supplies the wonderful texture that makes baba ghanoush such a treat.

1 eggplant, cut into strips

3 tablespoons (45 ml) olive oil, divided

2 ounces (55 g) bittersweet chocolate

4 garlic cloves, peeled

2 tablespoons (30 g) tahini

¼ cup (60 ml) lemon juice

1 tablespoon (15 ml) balsamic vinegar

1 teaspoon smoked paprika

2 teaspoons chopped fresh marjoram or oregano

½ teaspoon salt (or to taste)

Preheat the oven to 400°F (200°C, gas mark 6).

Place the eggplant on a baking pan and combine with 1 tablespoon (15 ml) of the olive oil and a little salt. Roast, turning once, for 30 minutes. Remove from the oven and allow to cool for about 15 minutes.

Melt the chocolate in a double boiler or bain-marie over low to medium heat while the eggplant cools. It will only take 5 minutes or so to melt your chocolate, probably less.

Next, blend all of the ingredients together in batches in a food processor, including the chocolate and eggplant, and transfer into a bowl. Allow the mixture to cool to simply warm if it is still very hot. Adjust the seasonings to taste.

This baba ghanoush is pretty delicious warm with pita and crudités, though chilled is also fine.

Yield: 3 to 4 cup-size (675 to 900 g) servings

Never-Fail Cocoamole

Here's an easy, rich recipe for parties. Avocado and chocolate are made for each other—they combine their fatty goodness conspiratorially. And that healthy fat in avocados works for you in more than one way—avocados increase the absorption of lycopene, the beneficial phytochemical found in tomatoes.

⅓ cup (27 g) unsweetened or bittersweet cocoa powder

3 avocados, pitted, peeled, and chopped

¼ cup (60 ml) lime juice, plus more to taste

2 teaspoons prepared mustard (Dijon or spicy brown mustard are good; flavored is great, too—experiment!)

¼ cup (4 g) chopped fresh cilantro

2 teaspoons chopped jalapeño

2 to 3 tablespoons (28 to 45 ml) olive oil

¼ teaspoon salt, or to taste

¼ cup (45 g) chopped tomatoes

2 tablespoons (20 g) chopped onion

Blend all of the ingredients until smooth, adjusting the seasonings to taste. Blend in a food processor for a smooth texture, or, if you prefer chunkier guacamole, mix with a spoon by hand in a bowl—in which case, mash the avocado, cocoa, and lime juice together first before adding the other ingredients. Of course, you may also use melted chocolate to make this instead of the cocoa powder for a different taste and texture. Decorate with cilantro, shaved chocolate curls, and perhaps jalapeño rings and avocado and tomato slices for a creative appearance.

Yield: 3 cups (675 g)

Basic but Wholly Scrumptious Fudge

This recipe has considerably less sugar than most fudge, and the coconut packs those beneficial medium-chain fatty acids that make it a popular alternative to dairy.

2 cups (350 g) bittersweet or dark chocolate chips

1 cup (235 ml) thick coconut milk

2 tablespoons (28 g) coconut oil

1 teaspoon vanilla

½ cup (60 g) chopped walnuts, (55 g) pecans, (50 g) almonds, or other nut

Melt the chocolate chips and coconut milk and oil in a double boiler, stirring occasionally. Add the vanilla and remove from the heat. Stir in the nuts. Pour into a greased glass baking dish (6 × 6 inches [15 × 15 cm] for thicker pieces, 8 × 8 inches [20 × 20 cm] for a little thinner). Refrigerate until set. Cut into squares.

This recipe makes about 3½ cups by volume; the number of pieces depends on how you choose to cut it. If you decide not to cut it and have it be one gigantic piece of fudge, please contact me because you're my type of fudge fanatic!

Yield: 12 pieces

Delicious, Judicious, and Nutritious Juice with Cacao

Wouldn't we be remiss to not have some juice in here for you to enjoy? This recipe is tangy and sweet, and secretly even more beneficial with that kale (full of vitamins A and C, calcium, iron, and folic acid) in there. Honestly, you can add cacao to any juice recipe that you enjoy, and you'll be the happier for it. Experiment!

4 cups (500 g) chopped apples

2 cups (250 g) chopped pears

1 cup (155 g) pitted cherries

½ cup (48 g) chopped fresh ginger

2 cups (134 g) chopped kale

Water, as needed, for thinning

⅓ cup (32 g) raw cacao powder

1 tablespoon (15 ml) lemon juice

Sweetener of choice, to taste (optional)

Add all the ingredients except the cacao powder, lemon juice, and sweetener to a juicer and combine. Blend the cacao into the juice using a regular or immersion blender. If you have fast hands, you can also beat it in with a whisk. Stir in the lemon juice and sweetener to taste. Serve.

Yield: 4 servings

Stunning Raw Cacao–Veggie Four-Layer Stack

This recipe is fairly complex in flavor but simple to make. Raw cacao can be combined with a number of vegetables to achieve your desired effect. Walnuts are an underrated source of those beneficial omega-3 fatty acids, and cauliflower is part of the super-healthy cruciferous family that includes broccoli, cabbage, and kale. These cancer-fighting vegetables should be eaten every day, and here's a fun, chocolaty way to get them.

½ cup + 2 tablespoons (48 g + 12 g) raw cacao powder, divided

1 cup (100 g) shelled walnuts

3 peeled garlic cloves

4 tablespoons (60 ml) lemon juice, divided

2 tablespoons (5 g) fresh sage leaves

Sea salt, to taste

1 cup (67 g) chopped kale

2 tablespoons (20 g) chopped red onion

2 teaspoons cider vinegar

1 cup (150 g) diced bell pepper

½ cup (73 g) shelled sunflower seeds

1 cup (100 g) chopped cauliflower

¼ cup (60 g) raw tahini

Put ⅓ cup (32 g) of the cacao powder, the walnuts, garlic, 2 tablespoons (28 ml) of the lemon juice, sage, and salt in a blender or food processor and process until it is the texture of pesto. Set aside in a bowl.

Place the kale, onion, cider vinegar, and a little salt in the blender or food processor, grind, and set this aside in a separate bowl. Next, purée the bell pepper, sunflower seeds, the rest of the cacao, and salt to taste until smooth and set aside in a third bowl. And finally, blend the cauliflower, tahini, salt to taste, and the rest of the lemon juice (you can add yet more cacao to this if you wish).

Stack each blend on top of one other in whatever order you fancy to make 4 layers, dividing among 4 plates. Chop any leftover ingredients to garnish and decorate.

Yield: 4 servings

Raw Spaghetti Squash–Cacao Nests

The interesting texture of spaghetti squash, here used raw, is playful with the rich deep flavor of cacao. If you've never had it, the inside of this squash really does resemble spaghetti! And at only 30 calories per cup (101 g), it's a fun, vegetable-based alternative to wheat pasta with significantly fewer calories.

About half a medium spaghetti squash (to equal 2 cups [202 g] of the flesh)

2 peeled garlic cloves

⅓ cup (32 g) raw cacao powder

½ cup (28 g) chopped sun-dried tomatoes

½ cup (90 g) fresh chopped tomato

2 tablespoons (8 g) fresh oregano

⅓ cup (42 g) dried olives

¼ cup (33 g) chopped carrot

¼ cup (40 g) diced onion

2 tablespoons (8.8 g) pumpkin seeds

½ cup (20 g) basil leaves, cut into ribbons

1 teaspoon lemon juice

1 teaspoon minced preserved lemon

1 teaspoon oil of choice

Sea salt, to taste

Remove and discard the seeds and goop from the squash half and pull the shreds out using a fork; it automatically gives you a cool stringy shape.

In a food processor or blender, blend the garlic, cacao, sun-dried tomatoes, tomato, oregano, olives, carrot, onion, and pumpkin seeds with sea salt, to taste, and a little water if necessary until nice and saucy (or to desired texture). Set aside.

Toss the basil with lemon juice, lemon, oil, and salt in a small bowl and set aside.

Toss the spaghetti squash with a little salt and any other desired spices or herbs (nuts can be nice as well) and place nests of it on plates. Use a scoop to do this or a fork to twirl a hole in the middle. Spoon some of the cacao mixture onto each "nest" and top with the dressed basil leaves. Serve.

Yield: 4 servings

Super What? The Powerful Benefits of Cacao

Cacao is no ordinary food, and the scientific community has taken note. From 2000 to 2012 alone, more than seventy human intervention studies were done on components of cacao in a variety of journals from around the world. And this doesn't include the plethora of lab studies on one or more of the 300 chemical compounds found in cacao. This research has looked at cacao's effect on everything from cholesterol levels to stress and even exercise recovery.

What makes cacao so special? Much of the research focuses on the powerful phytochemical group known as flavonoids, of which cacao is one of the best sources in the world. It has more than tea and wine, two foods often touted as superfoods for their flavonoid content alone. However, in cacao, flavonoids are far from the only beneficial compounds! Cacao is also a rich source of a variety of nutrients that may work synergistically with phytochemicals like flavonoids.

Cacao: A Nutrient-Dense Superfood

The most traditional way to evaluate the health of a food is to look at the nutrient levels. It is common practice to evaluate whether it is high in fiber (good!), contains few nutrients (less good!), or high in saturated fat (usually bad!) so recommendations on consumption can be made. Even when talking about superfoods, we want to see the big picture and understand best how they can fit into our diet. Fortunately, cacao is more than a phytochemical powerhouse; it is also a source of fiber, healthy fat, and minerals such as copper, magnesium, and iron.

Fiber by the Spoonful

The recommendation for fiber in the United States is 25 to 35 grams per day, and cacao beans, cacao powder, and dark chocolate can supply significant amounts. A 1-ounce (28 g) serving of chocolate has between 1 and 6 grams of fiber. Cocoa powder retains much of the fiber from the cacao bean and has about 2 grams of fiber per tablespoon (5 g).

Fiber has a number of functions in our digestive systems from slowing gastric emptying to easing elimination. Researchers in New Zealand recently analyzed diet patterns, looking for foods that are healthy, low cost, and environmentally sustainable. High-fiber foods were an important part of their conclusion and with reason: Increased fiber consumption is inversely related to risk of a number of diseases, including coronary heart disease, type 2 diabetes, and cancer.

Fat: The Misunderstood Nutrient

Fat sure can be confusing. Remember when all of those health recommendations said to eat a low-fat diet? Or the nonfat diet trend? All of those items filled with refined foods and sugar didn't help anyone lose weight or get healthier. The truth is, we need fat. We need it to properly absorb vitamins and keep our bodies functioning. Even minimal amounts help us feel satiated, bring out the flavor of food, and help make other foods more palatable. You know the wonderful feel of a good chocolate bar melting in your mouth? You can thank the fat content of the cacao bean for that.

So why the bad rap for fats? There are a couple of reasons. One is because fat has more than twice the number of calories per gram than carbohydrate or protein. An avocado and an apple may be the same size, but the avocado has more than twice as many calories. Another way to say this is that foods high in fat are calorically dense. Cacao is no exception: The fat and calorie contents have kept many people from enjoying it more often. But that doesn't have to be the case! Fat, especially plant-based fat, can be part of a healthy diet as long as you take the total calories you consume into consideration. The majority of the calories in cacao come from fat. A 1-ounce (28 g) serving of dark chocolate has about 12 grams of fat, which accounts for roughly two-thirds of the calories.

Not All Fats Are Created Equal

In addition to quantity, we have to consider the quality of the fat we consume. The majority of the fat found in cacao is saturated fat, long deemed unhealthy, but with exceptions that apply to cacao. About one-third of the fat content is monounsaturated, the type found in olive oil. Monounsaturated fat is associated with health benefits such as reduced LDL or "bad" cholesterol levels. These beneficial fats are found predominantly in plant foods such as olive oil, avocado, and nuts and are often recommended as part of a healthy diet.

Saturated fats are usually not recommended because of their link to increased LDL cholesterol levels. But saturated fat and its effect on health is a rather complex scenario. For one, not all saturated fatty acids raise cholesterol levels. Stearic acid, the predominant saturated fat in cacao, is the exception! Current research says at worst it is neutral on LDL cholesterol and at best may even lower it. Additionally, some research has called into question the theory that saturated fat is a risk factor for cardiovascular disease at all.

Healthy Minerals—from Chocolate?

Minerals are inorganic chemical elements that come from the earth, and some are essential for the most basic human functions. Minerals make up our bones, teeth, and part of our blood and other bodily fluids. This may surprise you, but cacao is a good source of certain minerals. And these minerals may behave differently (and more beneficially!) in cacao by working with and protecting the antioxidant compounds that chocolate is known for. Let's take a closer at them.

- **Copper.** A 100-calorie piece of dark chocolate can contain as much as one-third of the Recommended Daily Allowance (RDA) of copper. Cocoa powder can contain about 20 percent of the RDA in just 1 tablespoon (5 g). Copper's most important roles are related to hemoglobin, iron, oxygen handling, and the release of energy. It also has a function with an enzyme that helps to prevent free-radical damage, similar to what antioxidants do. There is speculation that copper may work synergistically with phytochemicals, and that may partly explain the benefits of cacao. Copper deficiency, though rare, can lead to hypertension, inflammation, glucose intolerance, and hypercholesterolemia.

- **Magnesium.** Dark chocolate can provide about 10 percent of the RDA for magnesium in a 100-calorie serving. Raw cacao has even more—up to 25 percent of the RDA! Magnesium is found in our bones, muscles, heart, soft tissue, and bloodstream and is the fourth most abundant mineral in the body. It's active in the operation of more than 300 enzymes and works with calcium to keep the muscles functioning properly. It is often lost during the processing of foods, so as is often the case, whole foods are better sources of magnesium.

Although symptoms of magnesium deficiency are rare in the United States, it is estimated that most people do not meet recommendations. This could have negative impacts on your health, as magnesium is involved in protein synthesis, muscle relaxation, and energy production and is hypotensive. Deficiency is also associated with metabolic syndrome and insulin resistance, as we'll learn more about in chapter 4.

- **Iron.** We need iron every day for our red blood cells to carry oxygen and nutrients to our cells. The well-known deficiency, anemia, has side effects that include fatigue and malaise. Luckily, iron is found in abundance in plant foods like cacao. A 1-ounce (28 g) dark chocolate bar can have about 20 percent of the RDA for iron, which makes it a very good source! Raw cacao has even more.

A very important consideration with iron is absorption. Plant foods contain nonheme iron, which is less well absorbed than heme iron, found in foods from animals. Fortunately, we can increase absorption by combining good sources of iron with vitamin C–containing foods. This is common with chocolate, as it is often paired with fruit. With raw cacao, we are fortunate in that it contains some vitamin C already.

Phytochemicals and Antioxidants: Where Cacao Shines

It's terrific that cacao contains so many nutrients, but good nutrition is much more than just getting all of the nutrients in the right amounts. Instead of just filling a requirement, certain foods have additional health benefits. We have found that almost all of these foods with extra benefits come from plants, and cacao is no exception!

Phyto (meaning plant) nutrients are chemicals found in many plant foods that are believed to confer protective effects on health. They are different from vitamins and minerals in that they are nonnutritive; they are not essential to human health. There are no RDAs or specific public health recommendations for phytochemicals, but the research on the benefits of consuming plant foods rich in phytochemicals is strong. Literally thousands of phytochemicals have been identified! Often, foods with high amounts of phytonutrients are labeled as superfoods.

Antioxidants: Fighting Disease with Your Fork

Antioxidants are a type of phytochemical and are on the forefront of nutritional sciences. They are naturally occurring compounds found in plant foods, such as cacao, that scavenge the body for damage-inducing free radicals. Oxidative damage is associated with age-related diseases, cellular diseases like cancer, and cardiovascular diseases like heart disease. Additional good sources are berries, fruits, coffee, and wine. There is no daily recommendation for antioxidants yet, and the best way to get them is directly through whole foods.

Phytonutrients are found in almost all plant foods including cacao, fruits, vegetables, grains, legumes, nuts, seeds, spices, herbs, and in beverages like tea and coffee. Many act as antioxidants and protect the body from free-radical damage to cell membranes, DNA molecules, and other important areas and processes inside the body. Numerous vegetables and fruits are believed to have cancer prevention properties, in part because of their high antioxidant concentrations. Vitamins and minerals such as beta-carotene, vitamins C and E, copper, zinc, and selenium have antioxidant abilities in addition to their role as vital nutrients. The numerous categories of phytonutrients include the carotenoids found in dark leafy green vegetables, the sulfides in onions and garlic, the phytoestrogens in soybeans, and of course the flavonoids in cacao. Research continues to grow in investigating phytonutrient compounds, their mechanisms of action, and their relationship to health.

Cacao: Why It Is a Superfood

Cacao has more antioxidant activity than tea, wine, blueberries, or goji berries, which are the most common foods lauded for antioxidant-related health benefits.

Fruits and vegetables in particular are thought to be powerhouses for phyto-nutrients, and some like spinach, already plentiful in nutrients, are considered superfoods because of their additional phytonutrient content. In the fight against disease, these superfoods should be considered our front line of defense, as they are associated with health promotion and disease reduction in ways that combine with and complement vitamins and minerals. Cacao is considered a superfood because of its high concentration of these beneficial components in addition to its nutrient content.

Cacao is rich in flavonoids, a type of polyphenol. The amount of flavonoids depends on the amount of processing and manufacturing cacao undergoes, but cocoa powder can contain up to 10 percent of its weight in flavonoids. Flavanols are one of six compounds further classified as flavonoids. These are the compounds that separate cacao from other foods and unequivocally make it a super-food for life. Let's look at some definitions we'll be using throughout the book.

- **Polyphenols.** This large class of compounds includes flavonoids, isoflavones (found in soybeans), anthocyanins, and tannins. Also called phenolic com-pounds, they are often associated with wine and tea, where they are found in large amounts. Polyphenols are often broken down into two categories: flavonoids and nonflavonoids. Significant research on polyphenols, spanning numerous chronic diseases, shows consumption is beneficial.

- **Flavonoids.** This category of polyphenols includes flavanols (also called flavan-3-ols), anthocyanins, flavonols, and flavones.

- **Epicatechin.** This is the main flavonoid in the cacao bean and is studied extensively. This phytochemical has a variety of structures, and current research looks at how each one behaves in an attempt to isolate the most active form. For the sake of simplicity, when we refer to any of them we will just call it epicatechin.

Now that we know a little more about what makes up this superfood, we'll learn more about its specific effect on our health and how we can incorporate it into our diet.

Putting It into Practice

- Eating cacao or chocolate in savory dishes may be new to you, so we're going to start with some simpler recipes. Don't be intimidated! As we try new foods and recipes, our taste buds adjust. Don't hesitate to alter the amount of cacao in a recipe as you ease into making these foods.

- Combine cacao with vitamin C–containing foods such as bell peppers, broccoli, and citrus fruits to increase the absorption of the iron that cacao contains.

- Cacao can easily be combined with other phytonutrient-rich superfoods like quinoa, chia, and coconut both in recipes and in chocolate bars.

- Because cacao and chocolate are calorically dense, be sure to moderate the amount of fat and calories you use when you are cooking. Even if you are eating healthy foods, you can have too much of a good thing. Be mindful of nuts, seeds, added oils, and other dense sources of calories.

- Eat more fruits and vegetables! These are the phytochemical powerhouses and should make up a large portion of each meal. A serving size of cooked vegetables is only ½ cup; getting "five a day" then is only 2½ cups of cooked veggies a day. The following plant-based recipes combine the power of cacao with phytochemical-dense vegetables to make healthy, unique, delicious meals at home!

CHAPTER TWO

Recipes at a Glance

Quinoa–Chocolate Chip Energy Bars

Here is an exciting and delicious use of quinoa with chocolate. You can vary the recipe with different combinations of grains, seeds, nuts, and dried fruit to suit your needs and tastes. Quinoa is prepared and used much like a cereal or grain, but it is actually a seed. It is high in protein, fiber, iron, and other minerals plus beneficial flavonoids, like cacao is.

1½ cups (260 g) uncooked quinoa

½ cup (48 g) ground almonds or other nuts

½ cup (43 g) grated dried coconut

½ cup (60 g) dried cranberries

½ cup (43 g) chopped dried apples

¼ teaspoon salt, or to taste

½ cup (130 g) cashew or almond butter

½ cup (160 g) agave nectar

¼ cup (56 g) coconut oil

½ cup (88 g) fruit-sweetened mini chocolate chips

Preheat the oven to 350°F (180°C, gas mark 4).

Spread the quinoa on a baking sheet and toast for 7 or 8 minutes. Remove from the oven, place in a large bowl, and add the nuts, coconut, and dried fruit. Set aside.

In a medium saucepan, combine the salt, nut butter, agave, and oil. Bring to a simmer over medium heat. Quickly remove from the heat. Pour over the quinoa mixture and combine until the dry ingredients are evenly coated. Mix in the chocolate chips. Spoon into a greased 9- × 13-inch (23 × 33 cm) baking dish. Press the mixture down into the pan. Bake for 15 minutes. Let cool and then cut and serve or store in an airtight container.

Yield: 12 bars

Raw Cacao Applesauce with Pumpkin Seeds

Apples are rich in antioxidants, and they're tasty, too! Pumpkin seeds add loads of fiber, iron, and magnesium and make for a more interesting textural experience by giving a little crunch to something that is normally smooth.

2 cups (250 g) chopped Granny Smith apples

2 cups (250 g) chopped apples (Braeburn, Honeycrisp, Gala, or Jonagold)

1 teaspoon fresh ginger

⅓ to ½ cup (32 to 48 g) raw cacao powder

¼ teaspoon salt

Scrapings of 1 vanilla bean

1 tablespoon (15 ml) lemon juice

2 tablespoons sweetener of choice, or to taste (optional)

¼ cup (35 g) raisins (optional)

¼ cup (57 g) shelled whole, chopped, or ground pumpkin seeds

Blend all but the pumpkin seeds in a food processor or blender until the texture is to your liking. Chill in a large bowl (or serving-sized bowls) in the refrigerator for an hour or two before serving. Sprinkle with pumpkin seeds.

VARIATIONS: Try using agave nectar or maple syrup for the sweetener. For the raisins, choose golden, regular, a mix, or dried berries instead.

Yield: 9 servings (½ cup [125 g] each)

Raw Kale in Chocolate-Orange Dressing

Here we have that trendy old kale, matched up with the soon-to-be even trendier chocolate! They should have been best friends all along! Kale ranks high in the nutrition department. It's not only loaded with calcium and iron, but also it provides protein and omega-3 fatty acids. Plus its antioxidant content is up there with berries and cacao—it is one of the healthiest foods you can eat.

2 to 3 tablespoons (14 to 21 g) raw cacao nibs

¼ cup (60 ml) orange juice

1 garlic clove

2 teaspoons olive oil

Salt, to taste

Lime juice, to taste

2 bunches kale, washed, ribbed, and chopped

¼ cup (57 g) shelled pumpkin seeds

½ cup (90 g) diced tomatoes, drained

½ cup (75 g) diced red or orange bell pepper

Chile flakes or minced chile pepper, to taste

Blend the cacao nibs, orange juice, garlic, olive oil, and salt. Add the lime juice. Toss with the other ingredients in a large salad bowl and allow to sit for 10 minutes. Then toss again, adjusting seasonings as needed.

Yield: 4 to 6 servings

One-Hour Mole

This mole takes like it should take all day when made from scratch, but is ready in an hour. This sauce is great for so many things—pair it with Wow! Chocolate Dinner Enchiladas (page 27), Relleno Poblano (page 84), or Cocoa-Potato Tacos (page 128). Tomatoes play a key role here. Well known for their vitamin C content, they are also a source of iron, vitamin K, and potassium. Tomatoes are low in calories, but 10 percent of those calories are from protein, surprisingly!

1 carrot

1 plantain, peeled

1 bell pepper, halved and seeded

6 garlic cloves in husks

1 onion, peeled and halved

2 to 3 tablespoons (28 to 45 ml) oil, such as olive or corn

3 or 4 dried and seeded ancho chile peppers

3 cups (700 ml) vegetable or mushroom broth, warmed, divided

1 cinnamon stick (2 inches, or 5 cm)

1 teaspoon whole cumin seed

1½ teaspoons whole coriander seed

2 tablespoons (16 g) sesame seeds

1 teaspoon peppercorns

1 cup (240 g) crushed tomatoes

1½ teaspoons chili powder

½ teaspoon salt, or to taste

2 teaspoons minced fresh oregano

2 tablespoons (28 ml) to ¼ cup (60 ml) chipotle sauce, or to taste

¼ cup (35 g) cornmeal

½ cup (18 g) toasted bread (optional)

½ cup (75 g) your favorite shelled roasted nuts

2 tablespoons (19 g) unpacked brown sugar or (40 g) agave nectar (optional)

4 ounces (115 g) unsweetened or bittersweet chocolate

¼ cup (4 g) chopped fresh cilantro

Preheat the oven to 450°F (230°C, gas mark 8).

In a casserole dish or baking pan, place the carrot, plantain, bell pepper, garlic cloves, and onion. Sprinkle with a little oil and salt and roast for 20 minutes, turning once. When finished, remove from the oven and allow to cool for 5 minutes.

While the vegetables are roasting, rehydrate the chiles in 1 cup (235 ml) of the broth for 10 minutes and then purée the mixture. Toast the cinnamon stick, cumin, coriander, sesame seeds, and peppercorns in a dry pan for 3 to 4 minutes over medium heat. Then crush them and grind them into a powder with a mortar and pestle or spice or coffee grinder.

Place the tomatoes in a large heavy pot with the rest of the broth, the ground spices, chili powder, salt, oregano, chipotle, ancho-broth purée, and cornmeal. Cook at a low simmer for the duration of the roasting time.

Peel the garlic and grind it and the rest of the roasted veggies in a food processor with the toasted bread and nuts and the remaining oil, if desired. Add to the tomato mixture in the pot and cook for 10 minutes, stirring here and there. Add the chocolate and cilantro and cook for 10 minutes more. Adjust the seasonings to taste.

NOTES: You can cook the mole for another 10 to 15 minutes if you like. Add more broth or liquid to thin or add more cornmeal to thicken. Lime juice is a nice addition to brighten the taste if you feel it is too heavy. Also, you can toast the cornmeal with the spices if you wish, to add to the toasting and roasting party.

VARIATIONS: Customize this recipe by using your favorite nuts, such as almonds, pecans, hazelnuts, peanuts, pistachios, or a combination. Instead of the optional soft bread, use ½ cup (113 g) cooked potato or (136 g) sweet potato, or ¼ cup (35 g) extra cornmeal.

Yield: 6 to 7 cups (1.5 to 1.8 kg)

Easy but Memorable Quinoa Pilaf with Cacao Nibs

Cacao nibs are a fun taste and texture to add to pilafs—they really pop! And cacao isn't the only antioxidant superstar; blueberries supply the powerful phytochemical *anthocyanin*. There's promising research that blueberries have a beneficial effect on blood sugar. And quinoa is a delicious complete protein.

4 cups (740 g) cooked, drained quinoa

½ cup (178 g) crushed cacao nibs

1 cup (145 g) blueberries

½ cup (85 g) sliced strawberries

½ teaspoon salt, or to taste

1 to 2 tablespoons (15 to 28 ml) olive oil

2 tablespoons (28 ml) lemon juice

1 teaspoon grated lemon zest

¼ cup (16 g) chopped fresh dill

¼ cup (24 g) chopped fresh mint

4 ounces (115 g) chopped arugula

½ cup (45 g) roasted soy nuts (Seasoned are fine.)

½ cup (80 g) finely chopped red onion

A little pomegranate vinegar (optional)

Composing this pilaf is quite simple: Toss all the ingredients together in a large salad bowl and season to taste. Serve chilled or warm.

VARIATIONS: Use different berries or herbs, replace the soy nuts or add pecans, pine nuts, pumpkin seeds, or other tasty seeds or nuts to complement them. Also, you can add 1 to 2 cups (205 to 410 g) of chopped roasted squash or (245 to 490 g) pumpkin to make this a heartier pilaf. There are so many choices!

Yield: 4 main or 8 side servings

A Very Special Waldorf-Style Salad

It's easy to make a version of this classic salad with pieces of chocolate combined with other tasty and beneficial ingredients. Strawberries may be a common fruit, but their benefits are anything but. They have more antioxidant capacity than blueberries!

½ cup (75 g) golden raisins

½ cup (60 g) diced celery

½ cup (55 g) chopped pecans

½ cup (85 g) chopped bittersweet chocolate

½ cup (85 g) sliced strawberries

½ cup (65 g) diced jicama

1 diced apple (I'm a fan of sour varieties, such as Granny Smith.)

2 satsuma oranges, seeded, peeled, and separated into wedges (or use another type of orange or a small tangerine)

2 tablespoons (8 g) minced fresh parsley, preferably Italian

1 tablespoon (6 g) minced fresh mint

Salt and black pepper, to taste

1 tablespoon (15 ml) apple cider vinegar

1 tablespoon (15 ml) olive oil

Toss all of these delightful ingredients together in a large salad bowl and season to taste.

VARIATION: You can add a bit of Dijon mustard or horseradish for an interesting bite. I favor a light dressing for this salad because it allows the ingredients and their flavors, which are lovely of themselves, a chance to shine.

Yield: 2 main or 4 side servings

Addictive Stuffed Dates

These never fail to make an impression! They are a bit decadent, but of course dates are wonderful and provide vitamin A and tannins with antioxidant properties as well. And pecans, like walnuts, have naturally occurring plant sterols that lower total cholesterol levels.

¼ cup (28 g) chopped pecans

¼ cup (33 g) grated chocolate

½ cup (55 g) soy chorizo (or ½ cup [85 g] mashed, cooked fava beans mixed with 1 teaspoon chile sauce)

1 teaspoon balsamic vinegar

1 teaspoon olive oil

2 tablespoons (40 g) marmalade

Salt and black pepper, to taste

24 large pitted dates, slit along the top to be stuffed

2 tablespoons (6 g) minced fresh chives, divided

Mix all the ingredients except the dates and half of the chives in a medium bowl. Stuff each date with slightly less than 1 tablespoon (15 g) of the mixture.

Serve sprinkled with chives or place in a baking dish and broil until some tasty broiling marks appear (about 5 to 7 minutes) and then sprinkle with the chives.

NOTE: You can use any sort of date for this recipe. Note that Medjool dates are a bit sweeter than the amber-colored Noor and can also be a good bit larger.

Yield: 24 stuffed dates

Most Popular Stuffed Mushrooms

I get so many requests for these, and yet I never tire of making them because they're so delicious! You can vary the types of nuts and herbs to make a difference in both taste and nutritional value. Pine nuts contain useful levels of fatty acids as well as a whole troop of minerals (magnesium in particular). Cremini mushrooms also represent with a bit of potassium and selenium.

½ cup (70 g) pine nuts

¼ cup (33 g) grated bittersweet or dark chocolate

¼ cup (10 g) chopped fresh basil

2 peeled garlic cloves

2 tablespoons (20 g) chopped white onion

2 tablespoons (7 g) chopped sun-dried tomatoes

¼ cup (45 g) cooked mashed cannellini beans

1 or 2 tablespoons (15 or 28 ml) lemon juice or balsamic vinegar

1 tablespoon (15 ml) olive oil

Salt, to taste

12 big ol' cremini or button mushrooms, stems removed

Preheat the oven to broil.

In a large bowl, blend all the ingredients except the salt and mushrooms until they reach a coarse, pesto-like texture. Season to taste. Stuff each mushroom with about 1½ tablespoons (23 g) of the filling. Place in a lightly greased baking dish and sprinkle with a little oil. Broil until the tops are browned, around 5 minutes. Set them on a paper towel before serving to get rid of some of the excess water that comes from cooking.

NOTE: You can reserve the mushroom stems for another use, such as making broth.

VARIATIONS: These mushrooms are fine without broiling, if you like raw mushrooms. One thing you can do is put the stemmed mushrooms in a bag with a small amount of smoked or sea salt in the refrigerator for 2 or 3 hours or even overnight and they will cure a little, for a slightly less raw texture.

Yield: 12 stuffed mushrooms

Cocoa-Mango Lassi

Who doesn't love a lassi? It's a refreshing and nutritious yogurt drink, and chocolate is an obvious match. Mango adds vitamin C and beta-carotene, the precursor of vitamin A. How about strawberries, honeydew melon, or peach? The sky (or your imagination) is the limit! If coconut is not your milk of choice, others will work here as well!

½ cup (40 g) cocoa powder

2 or 3 tablespoons (40 or 60 g) sugar syrup or agave nectar, or to taste

1½ cups (355 ml) coconut milk with cream (or [345 g] coconut yogurt, even better!)

¼ cup (60 ml) lemon juice

Couple pinches salt

½ teaspoon cardamom

1 cup (175 g) chopped mango (Frozen works great.)

½ cup (120 ml) mango juice

Blend all the ingredients until smooth and add more liquid if needed for a drinkable texture. Season to taste. Pour over ice in tall glasses.

Yield: 2 large or 4 small lassis

A Super-Tasty Blueberry-Cacao Super Smoothie

Oats, cacao, and blueberries all have great nutritional properties and combine here for quite the super-tasty trio! Blueberries, in addition to their antioxidant content, are an excellent source of vitamin K, and oats contribute cholesterol-lowering soluble fiber.

½ cup (48 g) raw cacao powder

1½ cups (355 ml) oat milk

1 cup (145 g) blueberries

Scrapings of 1 vanilla bean

½ teaspoon ground cinnamon

1 banana

1 tablespoon (15 ml) lemon juice

Sweetener, to taste (optional)

Blend the ingredients together in a powerful blender and adjust the seasonings to taste. Chill before serving if you wish.

VARIATION: You can add 2 tablespoons (24 g) of flaxseeds for additional benefits. Flaxseeds are a terrific source of omega-3 fatty acids and are ideal because they contain more omega-3s than omega-6s. You can't say the same about many other foods! Omega-3 fatty acids are good for your heart, but the ratio of omega-6 to omega-3 we consume daily is equally important. A high omega-6 to omega-3 ratio may promote the development of many diseases, from cardiovascular disease and cancer to inflammatory and autoimmune diseases.

Yield: 2 servings

Cacao-Spice Mix for Sprinkling

Turmeric, one of the main ingredients in this blend, is well known for its curcumin content, the naturally occurring pigment that gives turmeric its characteristic yellow color. A 2007 study in *Advanced Experimental Medical Biology* concluded that curcumin exhibits antioxidant, anti-inflammatory, antiviral, antibacterial, antifungal, and anticancer activities. It gives this recipe a hint of curry as well. Experiment and use any blend of spices that excites you.

¼ cup (24 g) raw cacao powder

½ teaspoon salt

2 teaspoons turmeric

1 teaspoon paprika

1 teaspoon garlic powder

2 tablespoons (12 g) nutritional yeast

1 tablespoon (8 g) sesame powder

1 teaspoon or two of other spice you like such as ground ginger, cumin, ground fenugreek, or coriander

Place all the ingredients in a small jar, put the lid on, give it a few shakes, and store in the cupboard until needed.

SUGGESTIONS: Here is a blend that you can sprinkle on baked dishes such as lasagna or pizza, salads, soups, popcorn, or even toast for an additional cacao boost.

Yield: 8 servings

Heart-Healthy Cacao: Little Bean, Lots of Benefits

You don't need an advanced science degree to know the important role our hearts play in maintaining good health. The heart is a muscle roughly the size of your fist that pumps blood through our arteries, delivering oxygen and fuel to our cells. The word *cardiac* comes from the Greek word for heart and means "related to the heart." The heart works with the vascular system—our arteries, veins, arterioles, and capillaries. Collectively, they are called the cardiovascular system: the network of organs, tubes, and fluids making up the crucial delivery system for fueling and supporting every organ, tissue, and cell in our bodies.

It is no surprise then that the leading causes of death worldwide are related to the cardiovascular system. In the United States alone, more than 80 million people have at least one form of cardiovascular disease. These diseases claim more lives than the next four leading causes combined! We know a lot about their mechanisms of development and risk factors, and it is no surprise that many are related to diet and lifestyle.

Risk factors for heart disease include increasing age, male gender, and heredity. Although you can't change these risk factors, you can influence others. For instance:

- Don't smoke.
- Exercise regularly.
- Maintain healthy cholesterol levels.
- Manage diabetes, if you have it.
- Keep your weight in a healthy range.

Nutrition and lifestyle are the key components of maintaining good health and reducing risk. And plant-based, phytochemical-containing plant foods such as cacao are the best tools we have!

From polyphenols to fiber to an exceptional saturated fat, cacao and chocolate can be part of a solid nutrition plan to reduce your risk of heart disease. Additionally, more specific studies are related to other chronic diseases such as obesity, hypertension, and type 2 diabetes.

Keeping Cholesterol in Check with Cacao

High total cholesterol, high LDL or "bad" cholesterol, and low HDL or "good" cholesterol levels are high on the list of diet-related cardiovascular risk factors. Serum cholesterol labs are a very cool thing, if you think about it. We are able to measure components of our blood and quantify them in a way to measure risk of a disease we may or may not get in the future. And when we get this number, we are taught, hopefully, ways to improve it through diet and exercise. If that's not futuristic, I don't what is!

The National Institutes of Health, through the National Cholesterol Education Program, has the following recommendations for cholesterol levels:

Recommended Cholesterol Levels		
LDL Cholesterol	**Total Cholesterol**	**HDL Cholesterol**
< 100 optimal	< 200 desirable	< 40 low
100–129 near optimal	200–239 borderline high	≥ 60 high
130–159 borderline high	≥ 240 high	
160–189 high		
≥ 190 very high		

The good news is that all three of these numbers—total cholesterol, LDL cholesterol, and HDL cholesterol—are greatly affected by diet. And the nutritional makeup and beneficial compounds in cacao can change them all for the better.

Lowering LDL Cholesterol and Raising HDL Cholesterol

Cacao is very high in the phytonutrient group called *polyphenols*. Specifically, it is a very good source of flavonoids that include catechin, epicatechin, and procyanidin. One way researchers test just how beneficial these polyphenols are involves using polyphenol-free cocoa powder control groups.

For example, one double-blind study published in 2007 in the *Journal of Nutrition* used multiple cocoa drinks: One had all of the polyphenols removed, while the others contained all the naturally occurring components in varying degrees. What researchers found was remarkable. For each of the polyphenol-consuming groups, LDL cholesterol levels dropped significantly after four weeks. And the results were even better for the individuals in the study who had high LDL cholesterol levels at the beginning of the study. Not only did their LDL cholesterol drop significantly, but their HDL cholesterol went up!

There are a number of possible explanations for why cocoa had this effect. For instance, atherosclerosis is the thickening of arterial walls from the accumulation of cholesterol and triglycerides responding to lesions and chronic inflammation. The collected fatty acid matter is known as plaque, and often atherosclerosis is referred to as hardening of the arteries. It is promoted by LDL cholesterol, which is why it is such an important biomarker of health. When we measure LDL cholesterol, we are looking to see how much plaque is built up on the main arteries. On the other hand, HDL cholesterol works to remove plaque, and therefore, we want our HDL levels to be higher.

The flavonoids in cacao have antioxidant properties that may protect the lipids and cells involved in the development of atherosclerosis from inflammation and oxidative damage. This would explain the inverse relationship between flavonoid intake and development of heart disease. And the flavonoids in cacao may also work synergistically with antioxidant-capable nutrients such as vitamin C and selenium.

Cacao: Full of Heart-Healthy Fiber

Fiber is an indigestible component of all plant foods and has no calories, despite being listed under carbohydrate on the nutrition label. There are two types of fiber. Soluble fiber is water soluble and slows the passage of food through the gastrointestinal tract. There is clear evidence that soluble fiber lowers total and LDL cholesterol. Insoluble fiber is not water soluble and has a bulking effect. The recommendation in the United States is 25 to 35 grams of total fiber per day, and the average American gets only about half of this amount.

The bran of the cacao bean is very high in fiber. Less-refined cacao products contain significant amounts of this important cholesterol-lowering nutrient. Whole cacao beans and cacao powder still contain the bran component and are definitely the best choices for fiber. Post-processing, the cacao solids used for chocolate bars do contain less, but they can still be considered a good choice.

Why You Should Read the Label When It Comes to Trans Fat

Created by chemically pumping hydrogen into oils to make them shelf stable, trans fats mimic saturated fats in both culinary use and negative effect on cholesterol levels. They are found in some types of margarine and many commercially packaged baked goods.

Trans fats do not naturally occur in plant foods, and cacao does not contain any trans fatty acids. This does not mean that all chocolate products are trans fat free, because baked goods, desserts, cookies, and so on are the most common source of these fatty acids. It's important to read the label to know for sure, looking for "hydrogenated oil," and to seek out the more whole-foods versions and dark chocolates.

A 1-ounce (28 g) serving of cacao has about 4 grams of total fiber, which is more than 25 percent of what the average American gets in one day! That's not too bad. For a lower-calorie option, cocoa powder isn't too shabby either when it comes to fiber, weighing in with 2 grams per tablespoon (5 g) in only 12 or so calories. The predominant form of fiber in cacao is insoluble but still adds to the equally important total fiber consumption in a day.

An Exceptional Saturated Fat

Saturated fat consumption has been linked to increased cholesterol levels and therefore increased risk of heart disease. Because of this, it has been given a bad rap. Saturated fat is found primarily in animal products, and this is the reason that health professionals recommend eating less meat, eggs, and full-fat dairy. Dietary saturated fat raises cholesterol levels more than dietary cholesterol.

But like anything, there are some exceptions, and one of them is crucial to understanding the benefit of cacao. The cacao bean is high in saturated fat, but one-third of the saturated fat is from a specific fatty acid called stearic acid. Guess what? Stearic acid is the exception to the rule! Enough research has been done to isolate this fatty acid and show it has no effect on cholesterol levels. This also leads to confusion when cacao and chocolate are discussed. Specific fatty acids are not listed on the nutrition label. All too often someone who knows a bit about nutrition will see the high saturated fat content and dismiss cacao as unhealthy. Fortunately, they will be wrong! If there is one take-home message from this chapter, it's that the saturated fat content in chocolate is not associated with an increased risk of cardiovascular disease because of its high percentage of stearic acid.

Phytochemicals Do the Prevention Work

As we learned in the previous chapter, phytochemicals are the future of nutrition and the key to preventing chronic disease. The extremely high phytochemical content of cacao makes it a very appealing food for research. And who doesn't like to hear good things about something we love? These phytochemicals operate in a number of ways that improve our cardiovascular function and reduce our heart disease risk. For example, the endothelium is the very thin layer of cells that lines the inside of our blood vessels. It has an important role as a selective barrier between the bloodstream and the surrounding tissue. Endothelium dysfunction is associated with, or caused by, several chronic disorders, including atherosclerosis. One way to test for endothelium dysfunction is to look at the flow-mediated dilation (FMD) of the arteries. One study looked at a number of flavonoid-containing foods and found that cocoa had the best results in improving FMD both short and long term. Even though the efficacy of using FMD to test endothelium dysfunction has been challenged, the results of this study are no less significant. The theory is that the flavonoids, specifically flavanol, have an anti-inflammatory effect and reduce platelet aggregation. They may also promote nitric oxide production, which has its own beneficial effect on vasoconstriction and vasodilation.

Putting It into Practice

- For the benefits of eating more fiber, choose whole cacao beans, cacao nibs, cacao powder, or dark chocolate.

- Soybeans and soy products such as tofu and tempeh can also help lower cholesterol levels and protect your heart. We've included recipes in this chapter that combine the benefits of cacao and soy into one healthy meal!

- Eating more fruits and vegetables is another way to reduce your risk of heart disease. Believe it or not, cacao goes very well with vegetables like eggplant, tomatoes, and mushrooms!

CHAPTER THREE

Recipes at a Glance

Rich Borscht with Cacao Accent

Beets and chocolate are great together, as they both have deep, earthy tastes that complement one another in this creative borscht. Firm and soft textures and a rich, silky broth combine for a luxurious experience. Beets are a unique source of the phytonutrient group called *betalains*. Betanin and vulgaxanthin, two examples of betalains, have anti-inflammatory and antioxidant properties. They are the source of the deep red color that beets, and borscht, are known for.

8 cups (1.9 L) vegetable, mushroom, or potato broth (or 8 cups [1.9 L] water mixed with 1 or 2 bouillon cubes)

1 to 1½ teaspoons salt

2 cups (220 g) diced potatoes

5 cups (1.1 kg) diced beets

½ cup (80 g) chopped red onion

½ cup (65 g) diced carrots

2 minced garlic cloves

1 teaspoon dill, or to taste

½ teaspoon paprika

½ teaspoon caraway or cumin seed, crushed

⅓ cup (32 g) raw cacao powder or to taste

2 to 3 tablespoons (28 to 45 ml) lemon juice

Chopped scallions, for garnish

Bring all ingredients, except the cacao powder, lemon juice, and scallions, to a boil in a large soup pot. Lower the heat to a simmer and cook for 20 minutes. Stir in the cacao powder and cook for another 20 minutes. Stir occasionally during this time.

Add the lemon juice and remove from the heat. Serve with the scallions and any other accompaniments you wish.

VARIATIONS: Mix up the ingredients for this soup by adding 1 cup (90 g) chopped cabbage, 1 minced chile pepper, 1 cup (70 g) sliced mushrooms, or 1 cup (166 g) diced tempeh to the pot. Garnish with grated chocolate on each bowl before serving.

Yield: 8 servings

Rich Chocolaty Vegetable Tarts

I have to restrain myself from making these tarts every day. Each vegetable works well with chocolate by itself, but when used all together, this recipe is to die for! And don't forget about the benefits of basil! Like cacao, basil is rich in flavonoids that protect cells and fight free radicals. Just 1 ounce (28 g) of basil has nearly 1.5 times the daily value for vitamin K and high amounts of vitamin A. It even contains a significant amount of iron and calcium! Basil is an herb we will be hearing a lot more about in the future. For now, enjoy these rich, delicious vegetable tarts.

1 cup (70 g) sliced mushrooms

½ cup (80 g) thinly sliced onion

2 minced garlic cloves, or to taste

1 teaspoon tamari, or to taste

¼ cup (12 g) minced fresh chives

1 batch Do-It-Yourself Cocoa Piecrust (page 188), using half the sugar and ½ teaspoon garlic powder

2 cups (600 g) sliced artichoke hearts

½ teaspoon salt

12 basil leaves (more if they are small)

1 cup (180 g) sliced tomatoes or 12 thin slices, drained to remove excess water

1 tablespoon (15 ml) olive oil

3 or 4 ounces (85 or 115 g) chopped bittersweet or unsweetened chocolate

Juice of 1 lemon (optional)

Preheat the oven to 425°F (220°C, gas mark 7). Lightly grease a 12-cup muffin tin.

Mix the mushrooms, onion, garlic, tamari, and chives together in a bowl. Set aside.

Divide the dough into 12 little balls, roll out into thin crusts (⅛ to ¼ inch [3 to 6 mm] thick) on a floured board, and press into the muffin tin. In each crust, place an equal portion of artichoke followed by an equal portion of mushroom mixture on top. Sprinkle with a little lemon juice if you wish and salt. Next, add a basil leaf, then a tomato slice, and finish with chocolate pieces and a sprinkle of olive oil.

Bake for 12 minutes, reduce the temperature to 375°F (190°C, gas mark 5), and cook for 15 minutes more or until the crust is done to your liking.

Yield: 12 servings

Chocolate-Cocoa Za'atar Pesto Balls

This interesting snack plays with a sweet-savory axis where the balance can be tipped in several directions. If you don't like one ingredient, try something different with a similar texture. Nuts, seeds, and herbs can be intermingled in different combinations to bring out varied nutritious aspects of this dish. Za'atar has several variations, but generally it is dried oregano, sesame seeds, and sumac powder, sometimes with garlic, olive oil (if it is in paste form), salt, chile flakes, and other herbs mixed in. The taste can be quite pronounced and takes some getting used to. It is easy to find in bags in the spice section of a Middle Eastern grocery or a large natural foods supermarket. The mixture's popularity is constantly increasing.

½ cup (48 g) ground almonds

½ cup (55 g) ground toasted pecans

2 teaspoons ground toasted sesame seeds

⅓ cup (43 g) grated dark chocolate

2 or 3 tablespoons (28 or 45 ml) olive oil

1 tablespoon (15 ml) lemon juice

⅓ cup (59 g) chopped pitted dates

¼ cup (15 g) chopped fresh parsley

2 tablespoons (6 g) minced fresh chives

2 minced garlic cloves

¼ teaspoon salt, or to taste

¼ cup (32 g) dry za'atar mixed with 1 tablespoon (5 g) cocoa powder and a dash of salt (salt optional)

Combine all the ingredients except the za'atar and add more liquid if necessary to be able to form into 16 to 20 small, firm balls. Roll the balls in the cocoa za'atar and chill until 5 minutes before serving or for at least half an hour.

NOTES:

- You can use cacao powder instead of the grated chocolate. If doing so, you will need to add about 2 tablespoons (22 g) more dates.

- If your za'atar does not have sumac powder in it, try to get some and add 1 tablespoon (6 g) of that to the recipe.

- If your za'atar already contains salt, you can omit the dash of salt called for.

Yield: 5 servings

Tasty Cocoa Jerk Tofu

Not too spicy and full of flavor, cacao makes magic with Caribbean cuisine! Soybeans are full of isoflavones, the phytochemical that may be responsible for soybeans' ability to lower cholesterol and reduce cancer risk. When you combine them here with cacao, you have a powerful phytochemical plate!

FOR THE SAUCE:

2 teaspoons curry powder

1 teaspoon chili powder

½ teaspoon each black pepper, cinnamon, and allspice

2 tablespoons (28 ml) hot sauce

⅓ cup (27 g) cocoa powder
(Use raw for a fattier, brighter flavor.)

¼ cup (60 ml) tamari

⅓ cup (80 ml) vegetable broth

2 to 3 crushed garlic cloves

1 tablespoon (20 g) agave nectar

2 tablespoons (28 ml) olive oil

1 tablespoon (15 ml) lemon juice or balsamic vinegar

2 tablespoons (32 g) hoisin or (38 g) plum sauce, (32 g) tamarind, or a similar sauce

½ teaspoon salt, or to taste

½ teaspoon ground oregano

FOR THE TOFU:

16 ounces (455 g) firm tofu

1 onion, sliced

1 red and 1 green bell pepper, each sliced

TO MAKE THE SAUCE: Blend together the sauce ingredients in a blender and set aside.

TO MAKE THE TOFU: Cut the tofu block into 4 sections and then cut each of these into 4 strips. Mix the tofu with the vegetables and sauce in a casserole dish or other flat-bottomed vessel and allow to sit for an hour.

Preheat the oven to 400°F (200°C, gas mark 6).

Add the tofu and bake, turning once, for 30 minutes, adding a bit more liquid if you need to or want this dish to be saucier. Increase the heat to broil and broil for 5 to 7 minutes to finish.

SUGGESTIONS: Serve this dish with seasoned black beans and rice. Some fried plantains would work well, too! Garnish with grated chocolate and scallions if desired.

Yield: 4 servings

Wonderful Wine Sauce

Wine and chocolate are wonderful together in so many ways, and both have gotten a bad rap in the past but are now revisited for their beneficial cancer-fighting phytonutrient content.

1 to 2 tablespoons (15 to 28 ml) olive oil

¼ cup (40 g) minced onion

2 minced garlic cloves

2 tablespoons (16 g) unbleached white flour

1 cup (235 ml) mushroom broth

1 cup (235 ml) red wine (Cabernet or Pinot Noir are recommended.)

⅓ cup (27 g) cocoa powder

2 tablespoons (28 ml) tamari or other seasoning sauce

¼ teaspoon black pepper

¼ teaspoon salt (optional)

1 teaspoon minced fresh sage

½ teaspoon smoked paprika

¼ cup (25 g) minced scallions or (12 g) chives

OPTIONAL ADDITIONS:
2 to 3 tablespoons (12 to 18 g) chopped fresh mint, ¼ cup (80 g) currant jelly, ½ cup (35 g) sliced mushrooms, ¼ teaspoon ground cloves

Place the oil in a medium saucepan over medium heat. Add the onion and garlic and sauté for 2 minutes.

In a small bowl, blend the flour into the broth and then add to the pan. Cook for 5 minutes. Add the other ingredients, except the scallions or chives, and cook for another 10 to 15 minutes until the sauce thickens, stirring occasionally. Add the scallions in when done.

SUGGESTIONS: Serve this sauce with mince pie or over grilled portobello mushrooms or roasted veggies or any other enticing dishes that beg a rich sauce.

Yield: 8 servings

Cancer-Fighting Cocoa Coleslaw

Coleslaw is versatile in both texture and composition. Red cabbage, part of the cruciferous vegetable group, is very high in polyphenols, especially the antioxidant, anti-inflammatory anthocyanins. And cabbage is probably best known for its glucosinolates, which are studied extensively for how they may help prevent some types of cancers.

1 tablespoon (15 g) prepared Dijon mustard

1½ tablespoons (25 ml) cider vinegar

1 tablespoon (15 ml) olive oil

2 teaspoons tahini

¼ cup (20 g) cocoa powder

½ teaspoon salt, or to taste

¼ teaspoon black pepper

½ teaspoon coriander, crushed

1 cup (70 g) shredded red cabbage

1 cup (70 g) shredded green cabbage

¼ cup (40 g) minced or grated onion

¼ cup (28 g) grated carrot

2 tablespoons (19 g) minced red bell pepper

2 tablespoons (8 g) minced fresh dill

Blend the mustard, vinegar, oil, tahini, cocoa powder, salt, and pepper in a small bowl. Add the coriander and reseason to taste. Toss with the other ingredients in a medium salad or mixing bowl and allow to sit for an hour either at room temperature or in the refrigerator before serving. Season again to taste before serving.

Yield: 6 servings

Decadent Choco-Spinach Lasagna

This is like mama never made! The full flavor of cocoa really is brought to life with the combination of tomatoes, balsamic vinegar, and spinach. Leafy greens, especially spinach, are an excellent source of iron that is extra absorbable when combined with the vitamin C of tomatoes. Garlic is more than an aromatic here; research shows it's as good for you as your grandmother always said thanks to its sulfur compounds, such as allicin, which have antibacterial and antiviral properties.

16 ounces (455 g) lasagna noodles, cooked

FOR THE SPINACH MIXTURE:

12 ounces (340 g) fresh spinach, chopped

4 minced garlic cloves

½ cup (80 g) chopped onion

2 tablespoons (28 ml) olive oil

Pinch of salt and black pepper

FOR THE TOFU MIXTURE:

16 ounces (455 g) crumbled firm tofu

1 teaspoon dried Italian herbs

1 teaspoon salt

2 tablespoons (28 ml) olive oil

1 tablespoon (15 ml) lemon juice

1 tablespoon (15 g) prepared mustard

2 tablespoons (10 g) cocoa powder

1 teaspoon garlic powder

FOR THE SAUCE:

28 ounces (785 g) crushed tomatoes

2 tablespoons (28 ml) balsamic vinegar

½ cup (48 g) cacao powder

½ teaspoon salt

2 minced garlic cloves

½ cup (20 g) chopped fresh basil

FOR SPRINKLING:

2 tablespoons (10 g) cocoa powder

2 tablespoons (12 g) nutritional yeast or "vegan Parmesan" sprinkle

¼ teaspoon salt

1 teaspoon garlic powder

½ teaspoon dried oregano

Preheat the oven to 375°F (190°C, gas mark 5).

TO MAKE THE SPINACH MIXTURE: Add all the spinach ingredients to a skillet and place over medium heat. Sauté for 3 to 4 minutes. Remove from heat, drain off water, and set aside.

TO MAKE THE TOFU, SAUCE, AND SPRINKLING MIXTURES: Combine all the tofu ingredients in a bowl, the sauce ingredients in another, and the sprinkling mixture in a third. Season all to taste and set aside.

In a 9- × 13-inch (23 × 33 cm) greased lasagna pan, spread a layer of crushed tomato sauce (about ½ cup [120 g]), followed by a layer of the noodles. Then spread all the tofu mixture on top, followed by another layer of noodles. Next, add the spinach mixture with a little more tomato sauce spread on top. Add another layer of noodles. Top with remaining tomato mixture and then the sprinkling mixture. Bake uncovered for 40 minutes. Allow to sit for 10 minutes before serving.

TIP: When using garlic, let it sit for about 10 minutes after you cut it and before you add it to heat. This protects the beneficial components from heat damage.

Yield: 10 servings

Relleno Poblano

Frankly, chile relleno ("stuffed peppers" in Spanish) should be a part of everyone's repertoire, partly because a pepper can be stuffed with just about anything, so experiment with this recipe. With mole, these are out of this world. I didn't fry or coat these in heavy breading or anything like that—this version is much simpler and highlights the sauce.

8 fresh poblano chile peppers

Olive oil for coating

1 cup (70 g) chopped mushrooms or (248 g) extra-firm tofu, (225 g) cooked sweet potato, or a combination

1 tablespoon (15 ml) chipotle sauce

¼ cup (20 g) cocoa powder (or raw cacao or pieces of chocolate)

½ cup (120 g) ground tomatoes

2 minced garlic cloves

½ cup (80 g) diced onion

Salt and black pepper, to taste

1 tablespoon (4 g) chopped fresh oregano

1 chopped bell pepper (red or green)

½ teaspoon ground cumin

1 teaspoon chili powder

2 tablespoons (28 ml) lemon and lime juice

½ cup (70 g) cornmeal with salt, 1 teaspoon garlic powder, and 1 teaspoon chili powder for coating

2 cups (500 g) Enchilada Sauce or One-Hour Mole (more if you like)

Preheat the oven to 400°F (200°C, gas mark 6).

Coat the peppers with oil (lightly) and place on a large baking sheet or pan. Roast for 30 minutes, turning once. Set aside until cool enough to handle. Slit lengthwise up one side. Remove the seeds, but leave the stems (for a more attractive presentation).

Mix the mushrooms through the lemon juice. Stuff the roasted poblanos, coat in light oil and seasoned cornmeal, and place in a large, greased casserole dish. Bake for 25 minutes. Serve with Enchilada Sauce (page 115) or One-Hour Mole (page 53).

SUGGESTIONS:

- Serve the enchilada sauce or mole warmed and on the side or poured on top of the chiles. Alternately, pour the sauce over the chiles and bake for an additional 10 minutes.

- You can remove the roasted pepper skins if you wish before stuffing. To do so, after the poblanos are done roasting, cool them in a paper bag first, which makes them easier to remove.

- Serve this dish with Mexican rice or quinoa for a heartier meal.

Yield: 8 servings

 DID YOU KNOW?

Poblano chiles are sometimes called pasilla chiles, but the two are different. Pasilla is actually the dried version of chilaca peppers, while dried poblanos are called ancho chiles—now you know! Both poblano and pasilla are so common now you see them everywhere interchangeably. They should be fairly large and dark green when compared to other chiles.

Chocolate and Roasted Squash Marinara for Pasta

This is a rich and hearty sauce matching squash (often an overly abundant vegetable in most people's gardens) with chocolate and wine. It's a bit of a magical trio there! Winter squashes are too often dismissed as just starchy vegetables, but they are off the charts when it comes to beta-carotene content. This compound is both a precursor to vitamin A and a powerful phytochemical. Additionally, oregano is more than a spice—it contains a fair share of nutrients and the phytonutrients thymol and rosmarinic acid.

3 cups (615 g) roasted butternut squash (or any similar squash, pumpkin, or kabocha)

2 cups (480 g) crushed tomatoes

¼ cup (60 ml) red wine

2 garlic cloves

½ cup (80 g) chopped onion

½ cup (55 g) grated carrot

1 cup (235 ml) vegetable broth (more as needed)

2 tablespoons (32 g) tomato paste

2 tablespoons (8 g) minced fresh oregano

½ teaspoon each ground cumin, coriander, turmeric, allspice, and paprika

Salt and white pepper, to taste

½ cup (66 g) melted bittersweet chocolate (or unsweetened if you prefer)

Blend all the ingredients except the chocolate in a large bowl. Transfer to a large pot and bring to a simmer, stirring occasionally, for 20 minutes. Add more liquid as needed or desired.

Mix in the chocolate, adjust the seasonings, and cook for an additional 10 minutes.

This sauce is great with any pasta or gnocchi, especially with shaved, unsweetened chocolate on top!

NOTE: If you ever make pasta or gnocchi from scratch, add some cacao powder! Yum, yum.

Yield: 8 servings

Fantastic Mince Pie with Cocoa-Wine Gravy

This is a fine dish if you want to impress someone. Endless combinations of vegetables and nuts can be used for this pie. And, of course, your favorite gluten-free crust with cocoa added can be substituted! Kale, nuts, and cacao combine for a vitamin- and mineral-packed trio of superfoods.

2 minced garlic cloves

½ cup (80 g) minced onion

2 tablespoons (28 ml) olive oil

1 cup (145 g) chopped nuts (Pecans, hazelnuts, or almonds are best!)

1 cup (150 g) total minced red and green bell peppers

1 cup (67 g) minced kale

1 cup (70 g) minced mushrooms

1 to 2 tablespoons (15 to 28 ml) tamari, or to taste

½ teaspoon black pepper

1 tablespoon (8 g) flour or (12 g) potato starch

½ tablespoon minced fresh oregano

½ tablespoon minced fresh rosemary

¼ cup (15 g) minced fresh parsley

⅓ cup (27 g) cocoa powder

1 batch Do-It-Yourself Cocoa Piecrust (page 172)

1 recipe Wonderful Wine Sauce (page 80)

Preheat the oven to 425°F (220°C, gas mark 7).

Add the garlic, onion, and oil to a large skillet over medium-high heat and cook for 2 minutes. Add the nuts, peppers, kale, mushrooms, tamari, pepper, flour, and herbs and cook for 5 minutes. Turn off the heat, stir in the parsley and cocoa, and adjust the seasonings. Set aside.

Roll out a top and bottom piecrust from the dough on a floured board to desired thickness. Press the bottom into a greased 9-inch (23 cm) pie pan (10-inch [25 cm] works if you prefer a skinnier pie).

Spoon the filling into the piecrust. Top with the other crust and crimp the edge. Brush with oil. Bake for 15 minutes and then reduce the temperature to 375°F (190°C, gas mark 5) and cook for another 20 to 25 minutes or until browned and done to your liking. Serve with Wonderful Wine Sauce.

Yield: 8 servings

Cacao: Super for Chronic Disease Prevention, from Obesity to Type 2 Diabetes

In the previous chapter, we discussed cacao's heart-healthy benefits. The research is very promising, and more will continue to emerge. But cacao is not only good for your heart—it has favorable effects on blood pressure, insulin sensitivity, and your risk of developing type 2 diabetes. Both studies that have followed people over time and ones that specifically tested the properties of cacao have shown very positive results in these areas.

High Blood Pressure, Hypertension, the Kuna, and Cacao

Hypertension is often called the silent killer because approximately one-third of those who have it do not know it. High blood pressure causes the heart and blood vessels to work harder and subsequently become damaged. Like cholesterol levels, high blood pressure can often be controlled or prevented through diet and lifestyle changes. Although having any cardiovascular disease is bad news, the good news is that you can change what you eat and reduce your risk of all of them. And including cacao in your diet is a good place to start.

To understand the connection between hypertension and cacao we have to go back to the research on the Kuna Indians of Panama. In 1997, Norman Hollenberg, MD, PhD, of Harvard Medical School, published a landmark paper in the research journal *Hypertension* that showed Kuna Indians older than sixty had no more hypertension than those between ages twenty and thirty. This paper inspired hundreds of studies, papers, and articles looking at the connection of cacao to human health, especially hypertension.

One study in the *Journal of Cardiovascular Pharmacology* hypothesized that the lower sodium intake of the Kuna, which is associated with lower rates of hypertension, was partially responsible, but concluded that this was not the main factor. According to the authors, the higher intake of cacao was the most notable dietary contribution to the unheard-of low rates of hypertension.

How Cacao Lowers Blood Pressure and Hypertension Risk

Cacao and its flavanols have a positive impact on endothelium function, as we've discussed in relation to heart disease. It turns out that many people have endothelium dysfunction because it's related to increased oxidative stress and reduced nitric oxide production. It is a caused by environmental pollution, tobacco use, lack of exercise, and poor diet. Good endothelial function widens blood vessels, which is also one of the pharmacological approaches in treating hypertension.

Dietary factors, including the consumption of cacao and dark chocolate, can also improve endothelium function. One review study in 2012 looked at twenty clinical trials on cacao and hypertension with 856 participants. The authors found a statistically significant reduction in blood pressure by 2 to 3 mm Hg in the short term in the cacao-consuming participants. They concluded that the flavanol content of cacao was responsible for the reduction. These studies looked only at short time periods and included varying amounts of cacao, but the research is promising that this superfood can lower blood pressure in both healthy adults and people with hypertension.

Type 2 Diabetes, Insulin Resistance, and Cacao's Antioxidants

An interesting and surprising research topic is the effect of cacao on type 2 diabetes. Diabetes is a disease in which an individual's blood glucose remains at higher levels than normal because of insulin insensitivity. Type 2 diabetes, previously called adult-onset diabetes, makes up the majority of diabetes diagnoses and is the seventh leading cause of death in the United States. Having diabetes is an independent risk factor for other cardiovascular diseases because the condition does significant damage to the cardiovascular system. The benefits of plant-based diets on the prevention and treatment of type 2 diabetes is well established.

A number of factors explain cacao's positive effect on type 2 diabetes. One, like hypertension, is related to diabetes and endothelium function. Hyperglycemia—having excess glucose in the blood, a trademark of diabetes—causes endothelial damage.

The flavanols in cacao increase nitric oxide production, which improves vasoconstriction and vasodilation—the narrowing and widening of blood vessels that controls blood flow. When the blood vessels are functioning properly, the endothelium is less susceptible to damage from diabetes. Additionally, epicatechin, a specific type of flavanol, may improve insulin sensitivity and reduce insulin resistance, inflammation, and oxidative stress in muscle and fat cells. These factors combine to reduce the significant negative impact type 2 diabetes has on the cardiovascular system.

Clinical studies that focus on the effect of cacao consumption on diabetes are not as numerous as they are for cacao and hypertension and other diseases. However, one such study concluded, "Diets rich in flavanols reverse vascular dysfunction in diabetes, highlighting therapeutic potentials in cardiovascular disease." It's worth noting that the Kuna Indians also have very low rates of type 2 diabetes.

The Magnesium in Cacao May Reduce Risk of Type 2 Diabetes and Hypertension

Cacao is a rich and underutilized source of the mineral magnesium. Magnesium is active in more than 300 enzymatic processes and is involved in protein synthesis, muscle relaxation, and energy production. RDAs for magnesium are 420 milligrams and 320 milligrams per day, for adult males and females, respectively. Although symptoms of magnesium deficiency are rare in the United States, most people do not meet these recommendations.

Two prospective studies that followed more than 170,000 health professionals, the Nurses' Health Study (NHS) and the Health Professionals Follow-Up Study (HFS), found that the risk of developing type 2 diabetes was greater in those with a lower magnesium intake. Magnesium is also an important mineral in the regulation of blood pressure. One review study observed that magnesium intake from foods is inversely related to blood pressure, but not magnesium from supplements. It's possible that the magnesium content of cacao could contribute to the observed health benefits of lower blood pressure.

Data from the Insulin Resistance Atherosclerosis Study showed that magnesium was positively associated with insulin sensitivity, another study indicated magnesium is inversely related to the development of metabolic syndrome, and last, another prospective study in Europe known as EPIC showed evidence that magnesium (along with fiber) reduces diabetes risk. As mentioned previously, there is reason to believe that the nutrients in cacao work synergistically with flavanols to fight disease in a way that is unseen when each component or mineral is taken on its own. That's yet another reason to eat whole foods such as cacao: Get your nutrients and phytochemicals together in one whole food package. Dark chocolate provides about 10 percent of the RDA for magnesium in a 100-calorie serving, and raw cacao has even more—an astounding 25 percent of the RDA.

Cacao and Metabolic Syndrome Prevention

Metabolic syndrome, also known as cardiometabolic syndrome or syndrome X, is a combination of risk factors that, when grouped together, can help predict risk of cardiovascular disease. These factors include abdominal obesity, abnormal cholesterol levels, high blood pressure, and elevated fasting glucose. If an individual has three of the four symptoms, he or she is diagnosed with metabolic syndrome. With diet and lifestyle changes, metabolic syndrome does not have to lead to a heart attack. Cacao can play a role in prevention because of its combined effect on cholesterol, blood pressure, and fasting glucose.

Criteria from the American Heart Association and the National Heart, Lung, and Blood Institute for metabolic syndrome includes the following:

- Elevated waist circumstance: men ≥ 40 inches (102 cm), women ≥ 35 inches (89 cm)
- Elevated triglycerides = 150 mg/dL
- Reduced HDL cholesterol: men < 40 mg/dl, women < 50 mg/dL
- Elevated blood pressure: > 130/85 mm Hg
- Elevated fasting glucose:> 100 mg/dL

A 2012 study in *BMJ* (formerly the *British Medical Journal*) estimated the effect of chocolate consumption on chronic disease for those with metabolic syndrome. Its preventive use is promising because it has beneficial effects on a number of the factors that lead to metabolic syndrome. The authors concluded the following:

"The blood pressure lowering and lipid effects of plain dark chocolate could represent an effective and cost-effective strategy for the prevention of cardio-vascular disease in people with metabolic syndrome (and no diabetes). Chocolate benefits from being by and large a pleasant, and hence sustainable, treatment option. Evidence to date suggests that the chocolate would need to be dark and of at least 60 to 70 percent cocoa, or formulated to be enriched with polyphenols."

Obesity, Calories, Cacao, and Confusion

Being overweight simply means carrying extra body fat, while obesity is defined as carrying excessive extra body fat. Together they are one of the leading causes of preventable death in the United States and a risk factor for numerous diseases and disorders.

Excess calories that are eaten are stored as energy in the form of body fat. Carrying extra body fat changes the way our bodies function and can impact our health negatively. But as we look closer, we find that overweight and obesity are rather complex and affected by many factors. The old adage of "a calorie is a calorie" may no longer be true. The common argument against eating cacao or chocolate is that it leads to weight gain and therefore should not be considered a health food, but the research shows a more complicated picture.

Often people say, "Weight loss is easy, just eat fewer calories," but that ignores our psychological, social, and environmental relationships with food. If it were that easy, then yes, being overweight or obese wouldn't be a problem. But we have complex relationships with food, and cacao is no exception.

Cacao, Chocolate, and Satisfaction

I had a client once who was struggling with weight loss. She had a very stressful, demanding job and limited time to prepare the healthy foods she knew she should be eating. And she ate emotionally. Chocolate cake was her weakness. Then one day she told me she had been substituting one small piece of very dark chocolate for her usual piece of chocolate cake. And you know what? It fulfilled her cravings. I estimated she ate 300 to 400 fewer calories per day, but her cravings were met and she felt satiated, with the same sense of satisfaction that she found when eating the chocolate cake.

Of course calories are only part of the equation. Substituting cacao meant she was eating a more whole food; less added fat, sugar, and calories; and she was getting the associated health benefits of cacao.

The satisfaction one gets from the components of chocolate and cacao may have an effect on more than our physiological system. We'll talk more about how cacao affects the brain, appetite, and our sense of hunger in the next chapter.

Cacao, in modern times, is eaten predominantly as a confectionary treat loaded with added sugar and fat. No wonder it has the bad reputation! But as we've learned throughout this book, the more added ingredients a food containing cacao has, the less cacao and beneficial components you are consuming. We need to get away from the association of cacao and confectionary when we talk about health benefits, especially obesity.

The studies on this subject are varied, but there is some evidence that eating cacao—and even chocolate—doesn't lead to weight gain. A National Institutes of Health–funded study at the University of California, San Diego, looked at the diets of more than 1,000 people via a food frequency questionnaire and categorized the subjects by body mass index (BMI). They found that those who ate chocolate more often were actually less likely to be overweight. This was even after they controlled for physical activity levels. The results are in line with previous findings related to cacao's positive effect on multiple metabolic functions.

On the other hand, a 2012 review study found that chocolate consumption was directly correlated to BMI in healthy adults; the more chocolate one ate, the higher the BMI. A caveat, though, is that this was not true for participants with previous existing conditions such as hypertension and type 2 diabetes. This group had adjusted their diet by eating more fruits, vegetables, and chocolate and did not have correlating increases in BMI. My take-home message from the studies we have so far is this: When combined with a healthy diet—one that includes numerous servings of fruits and vegetables each day—regular consumption of cacao is beneficial and does not lead to weight gain. Eat it, enjoy it, and reap the benefits; just remember that variety is key, and good health and a long life are bigger than one specific food.

Cacao and Chronic Disease: Where to Go from Here

In an issue of the American Heart Association journal, *Circulation*, Norman Hollenberg, MD, PhD, wrote an editorial about his research on cacao and chocolate and how the public has interpreted it. Interviews by the press regarding cacao far outweigh interest on any other studies of food and health. But he explains that most journalists and laypeople are not entirely happy to hear what he has to say about cacao. For example, cacao is beneficial when it comes to cardiovascular health, he explains, but turning that into clear, specific recommendations is not easy.

Also, the flavanol content of cacao can vary widely based on a number of factors, especially production. How much flavanol do different chocolate bars have? And how much cacao or flavanols do we need to get the benefits? He reminds us that we don't have these specific answers just yet.

Additionally, recommending chocolate with added fat and sugar as a health food is precarious. Like most researchers, he is careful about how his studies are interpreted. He finishes the article by saying that the evidence on cacao is clear: It is beneficial for reducing blood pressure, hypertension, and other cardiovascular diseases. We know this much and can use that information wisely by consuming dark chocolate, cacao nibs, and nonalkalized cocoa, which are most likely to have the highest flavanol content. It is yet to be determined exactly how much should be eaten, but the future is bright for cacao, and if you are reading this and making the recipes we have included, you are ahead of the curve.

Putting It into Practice

- Choosing very dark chocolate or cacao nibs is especially important to realize the beneficial components of cacao in the reduction of cardiovascular disease risk.

- No one food has the power to lower disease rates on its own, and cacao is no exception. Including cacao as part of a bigger plan that includes exercise, fruits, vegetables, and whole grains is your best bet for long-term health.

- Like other calorically dense foods that are health promoting, you may need to adjust your total caloric intake when adding cacao to your diet. There's no need to do strict calorie counting, but it is important to have an idea of how many calories are in the foods you are eating when you make changes to your diet. You can have too much of a good thing.

- There's a lot we still don't know about food choices and chronic disease. But we do know that eating more fruits and vegetables reduces your risk of all of them! We've provided many plant-based recipes with cacao to make it easier for you to get those vegetables in a delicious way.

- Eat slower. I can't emphasize this enough. It's as true when enjoying a high-quality dark chocolate bar as it is when eating a weekday dinner. Not only will you enjoy your food more, you will eat less. Two tips: Never put more food in your mouth while you are still chewing and wait a few moments in between bites. This will extend your mealtime, in a good way.

CHAPTER FOUR

Recipes at a Glance

Ghoulishly Delicious Goulash

This old saw is given a remake with chocolate, bringing it to the next level. An extremely versatile stew, you can add whatever veggies you please to increase the nutritional benefits.

FOR THE COCOA SOUR CREAM:

¾ cup (186 g) silken tofu or (180 g) coconut cream

2 tablespoons (28 ml) cider vinegar

1 tablespoon (5 g) cocoa powder

½ teaspoon salt, or to taste

½ teaspoon powdered mustard

1 tablespoon (15 ml) olive oil

FOR THE GOULASH:

1 cup (110 g) diced potato

1 cup (160 g) chopped onion

2 minced garlic cloves

2 tablespoons (28 ml) olive oil

28 ounces (785 g) crushed tomatoes

1 cup (150 g) seeded diced bell peppers

1 cup (150 g) seeded diced Hungarian peppers

1 cup (90 g) chopped cabbage

1 cup (70 g) chopped mushrooms, (248 g) tofu, or (166 g) tempeh

1 tablespoon (4 g) minced fresh herbs

1 tablespoon (7 g) paprika

½ teaspoon ground cumin

¼ teaspoon black pepper

½ teaspoon salt, or to taste

½ cup (120 ml) red wine or vegetable broth

1 cup (235 ml) vegetable broth

1 cup (105 g) uncooked brown rice pasta (optional)

3 ounces (85 g) chopped dark chocolate

(Continued on page 104)

TO MAKE THE COCOA SOUR CREAM: In a large bowl, blend all the ingredients until smooth. Refrigerate while making the goulash. Before serving, garnish with scallions or dill.

TO MAKE THE GOULASH: Sauté the potato, onion, and garlic in oil in a large pot for 5 minutes over medium heat. Add the tomatoes, peppers, cabbage, mushrooms, herbs, paprika, cumin, pepper, and salt. Cook for 5 minutes, stirring. Add the wine and broth and cook for 10 more minutes. Add the rice pasta, if using, and chocolate and stir until the chocolate is melted. Cook until the pasta is done, about 5 minutes, depending on the type you are using. You can add more liquid if you feel like it, but it should be pretty thick. Serve with the sour cream.

VARIATIONS:
- For the minced fresh herbs, try dill and rosemary.

- Use ¼ to ⅓ cup (20 to 27 g) cocoa powder or (24 to 32 g) raw cacao instead of the chopped chocolate.

Yield: 6 servings

Holy Pozole! Chickpeas and Chocolate

Hominy, chocolate, and chickpeas are yet another delightful combination. And chickpeas are good for you—one cup (164 g) gives you nearly half a day's worth of fiber and 20 percent of your iron. Pozole (also posole) is a thick, hearty stew that comes from Mexico, the backyard of chocolate's origination. You can use cacao or cocoa powder in this recipe instead, about ¼ to ⅓ cup (24 to 32 g or 20 to 27 g) or more to taste.

16 ounces (455 g) tofu or tempeh (or 2 cups [140 g] mushrooms or [220 g] potatoes), cut into ½-inch (1 cm) cubes

1 tablespoon (15 ml) each soy and hot sauce

2 tablespoons (28 ml) olive or canola oil, divided

1 cup (160 g) diced onion

3 minced garlic cloves

1 bay leaf

1 teaspoon salt

¼ teaspoon black pepper

2 cups (360 g) diced tomatoes

1 seeded minced hot chile pepper (more for a hotter taste)

1½ teaspoons ground cumin

1 teaspoon coriander, freshly ground if possible

1 tablespoon (8 g) chili powder

½ teaspoon ground cinnamon

6 cups (1.4 L) vegetable broth, divided

2 cups (330 g) cooked hominy

2 cups (328 g) cooked chickpeas

½ cup (75 g) diced green bell pepper

¼ cup (33 g) diced carrots

2 to 4 ounces (55 to 115 g) bittersweet or unsweetened chocolate

Garnishing options: cilantro, minced chile, diced red onion, scallions, lime wedges, strips of crispy tortilla or chips

Toss the tofu or tempeh with the soy and hot sauces in a medium mixing bowl. Sauté in a medium skillet in 1 tablespoon (15 ml) of the oil over medium heat, turning occasionally until browned, around 6 minutes. Set aside.

In a large, heavy pot over medium heat, sauté the other tablespoon (15 ml) of oil, onion, garlic, and bay leaf with the salt and pepper for 2 to 3 minutes. Add the tomatoes and spices and cook for 5 minutes more. Add 5 cups (1.2 L) of broth and the rest of the ingredients except for the tofu and chocolate. Stir and allow to simmer for 20 minutes.

Heat the remaining 1 cup (235 ml) of broth in a saucepan (or in a bowl in the microwave) over medium-low heat. Grate the chocolate into a separate bowl and then whisk into the warmed broth until incorporated. Stir into the pot with the other ingredients.

Add the tofu and cook for 10 minutes more. Remove the bay leaf. Put in bowls, garnish, and serve.

Yield: 8 servings

Green Beans Amandine with Dark Chocolate

This is quite a succulent treat with the chocolate just melted in there. Don't fear the almonds! Almonds are high in heart-healthy, cholesterol-lowering monounsaturated fats, like olive oil. The Adventist Health Study, a long-term prospective research study that followed tens of thousands of people, found a significantly reduced risk of heart disease for those who ate nuts. The best results were among people who replaced saturated fats with the healthy fats found in nuts, like almonds.

2 cups (200 g) green beans

½ teaspoon salt, or to taste

½ cup (46 g) sliced almonds

2 tablespoons (28 ml) olive oil

1 tablespoon (15 ml) Chocolate Balsamic Reduction (page 109) or balsamic vinegar

1 tablespoon (4 g) chopped fresh tarragon

2 ounces (55 g) chopped dark chocolate

¼ teaspoon vanilla

Sauté the green beans, salt, and almonds in the olive oil in a large skillet over medium-high heat for 2 minutes. Add the balsamic vinegar and cook for 5 minutes more or until the almonds are browning nicely. Remove from the heat and add the other ingredients. Serve warm.

Yield: 4 servings

Chocolaty Grits

This is an easy, likable rendition of the familiar comfort food, with the added nutritional benefits of cacao! Depending on the type you get, grits can be a source of iron and fiber. Parsley is an excellent source of vitamins A and C.

¼ cup (40 g) chopped onion

1 tablespoon (15 ml) olive or canola oil

1 cup (235 ml) vegetable broth

½ teaspoon salt

¼ teaspoon black pepper

⅓ cup (47 g) dry grits

2 ounces (55 g) bittersweet chocolate, chopped or grated

2 tablespoons (8 g) minced fresh Italian parsley

¼ cup (25 g) chopped scallions

Lemon wedges, for garnish

Sauté the onion in oil in a saucepan for 2 minutes over medium-high heat or until lightly browned. Add the broth, salt, pepper, and grits, lower the heat to medium, and cook at a simmer for 5 minutes. Remove from the heat and cover, allowing to sit for 2 minutes more. Stir in the chocolate.

Divide among 4 bowls and garnish with the parsley and scallions, with a lemon wedge on the side.

VARIATION: You can put half of the chocolate in the grits while cooking and add the other half for serving on top.

Yield: 4 servings

Three Easy-Peasy Cacao-Inspired Untraditional Dressings

Salads are a quick and convenient way to get your veggies and greens, but all too often they are covered with unhealthy dressings. Enjoy these cacao-inspired healthy alternatives with your favorite salads.

COCOA CAESAR

⅓ cup (80 ml) lemon juice

3 tablespoons (45 ml) olive or sunflower oil

2 tablespoons (10 g) cocoa powder
(Use raw for a fattier, richer flavor; use cooked for a deep and smooth flavor.)

1 teaspoon toasted rice powder, seaweed flakes, or ground toasted sesame seeds

¼ teaspoon salt, plus more to taste

1 peeled, crushed garlic clove

Blend all the ingredients until smooth in a blender or with a whisk in a small mixing bowl. Adjust seasonings to taste. Serve on romaine lettuce with croutons or whatever other salad you may enjoy.

Yield: 6 servings

CACAO-TOMATO VINAIGRETTE

¼ cup (60 g) puréed tomato

¼ cup (24 g) raw cacao powder

¼ cup (60 ml) cider or white balsamic vinegar

¼ teaspoon salt (more to taste)

¼ teaspoon black pepper

1 teaspoon minced onion

1 peeled, crushed garlic clove

2 tablespoons (28 ml) olive oil

Liquefy all the ingredients in a blender and adjust the seasonings to taste. Shake before using. This dressing can be stored in the refrigerator for several days.

Yield: 8 servings

CHOCOLATE-BALSAMIC REDUCTION

1 cup (235 ml) balsamic vinegar

1 to 2 ounces (28 to 55 g) bittersweet or unsweetened chocolate

Heat the balsamic vinegar in a small pot until it begins to boil, reduce to a simmer, and stir periodically. When about a quarter of the liquid has evaporated, add the grated chocolate slowly over the next few minutes, stirring throughout. When the liquid has been reduced by half (or more), the reduction is complete!

VARIATION: You can also reduce the vinegar first and then stir in the chocolate until it is melted and incorporated.

Yield: 8 servings

Full-of-Fava-and-Flavanol Chocolate Foul

Fava beans really ought to be more common in meals—as should chocolate. I love this one because it is another fine blending of spices, chocolate, and tomatoes. Fava beans provide a whopping 13 grams of protein per cup (170 g) and are nearly fat free!

2 cups (340 g) cooked fava beans

4 ounces (115 g) chocolate, preferably bittersweet, chopped or grated

2 cups (360 g) diced tomatoes

2 tablespoons (32 g) tomato paste

1 cup (235 ml) mushroom or vegetable broth

½ cup (80 g) diced onion

½ cup (75 g) diced bell pepper

½ teaspoon ground cinnamon

½ teaspoon ground coriander

1 teaspoon chili powder

1 teaspoon ground cumin

¼ cup (4 g) chopped fresh cilantro

1 tablespoon (15 ml) lemon juice

2 tablespoons (28 ml) olive oil

Salt and black pepper, to taste

½ teaspoon ground sumac (optional)

Place all the ingredients in a large pot over medium heat, reserving some cilantro, onion, and bell pepper for garnish. Bring to a simmer and cook for 20 minutes. Serve in bowls with the garnish on top and with pita bread and sliced radishes.

Yield: 4 servings

Tamarind-Chocolate Chili

This is an easy and tasty way to have a hearty chocolate stew. Lentils are a nutrition powerhouse, chock-full of protein and minerals, and are low cost, quick to cook, and extremely versatile! Enjoy them here with the additional benefits of cacao and vegetables.

2 cups (396 g) cooked lentils or other legumes

1 cup (248 g) chopped seasoned tofu or (166 g) cooked tempeh

½ cup (80 g) diced onion

1 cup (235 ml) vegetable broth (more as needed)

1 cup (240 g) crushed tomatoes

2 minced garlic cloves

2 teaspoons chili powder

1 teaspoon ground cumin

1 teaspoon minced ginger

⅓ cup (85 g) tamarind purée

1 tablespoon (15 ml) lemon juice or balsamic vinegar

1 tablespoon (9 g) minced chile pepper

½ cup (75 g) diced bell pepper

¼ cup (28 g) minced carrot

½ cup corn, (77 g) fresh, (82 g) frozen, or (105 g) canned

2 tablespoons (28 ml) tamari

½ teaspoon black pepper

⅓ cup (27 g) cocoa powder or 2 to 4 ounces (55 to 115 g) chopped dark chocolate

¼ cup (4 g) chopped fresh cilantro

Sweetener of your choice, to taste (optional)

Garnish options: diced red bell pepper, cocoa powder or crushed cacao nibs, minced scallions, chopped cilantro, chopped pineapple, diced onion

Cook everything except the chocolate and cilantro at a simmer in a large pot, stirring occasionally, for 25 minutes. Add more broth or water if needed to keep your desired texture. Add the chocolate and cilantro and cook for 10 minutes more.

Yield: 5 servings

Chocolate–Sweet Potato Baked Ravioli

This is a time-consuming but worthwhile recipe. The Cocoa Marinara Sauce is great with just about any pasta or polenta!

FOR THE DOUGH:

1 cup (125 g) unbleached white flour

1 cup (168 g) semolina flour

¼ teaspoon salt

1 teaspoon garlic powder

1 cup (235 ml) lukewarm water

1 tablespoon (15 ml) olive oil

Flour or semolina, for rolling

FOR THE FILLING:

1 cup (225 g) cooked mashed sweet potatoes

1 chopped avocado

¼ cup (43 g) chopped dark chocolate

½ teaspoon curry powder

2 teaspoons lemon juice

1 minced garlic clove

2 tablespoons (20 g) minced onion

¼ teaspoon salt (more to taste)

2 teaspoons olive oil

TO MAKE THE DOUGH: Mix the flour and semolina with the salt and garlic powder in a large mixing bowl. Gradually mix in the warm water and olive oil until a workable dough is formed. Knead briefly and form into a ball. Wet slightly and place in a covered bowl for an hour.

TO MAKE THE FILLING: In a separate medium mixing bowl, combine all ingredients and mix well.

TO ASSEMBLE THE RAVIOLIS: Preheat the oven to 400°F (200°C, gas mark 6).

Roll out the dough to ⅛ inch (3 mm) thick and cut into an even number of 2- × 2-inch (5 × 5 cm) squares. Feel free to do this in batches. Place a dollop of filling on half of the squares and top with the remaining squares. Cinch the edges closed with a pastry cutter or your hands (or a fork). Place on a greased baking sheet and brush lightly with a little oil and water. Bake for 7 minutes, turn, brush again, and bake for another 7 to 10 minutes or until browned. Really, these are more akin to itsy-bitsy empanadas or pierogi with thin crust.

Serve with the Chocolate Marinara Sauce (page 115).

Yield: 4 to 6 servings

Chocolate Marinara Sauce

6 cups (1.1 kg) chopped tomatoes

2 minced garlic cloves

½ teaspoon salt

¼ to ½ cup (20 to 40 g) cocoa powder (depending on taste)

2 teaspoons (28 ml) balsamic vinegar

¼ cup (28 g) grated carrot

½ cup (80 g) minced onion

2 teaspoons minced fresh oregano

1 tablespoon (3 g) minced fresh basil

¼ teaspoon black pepper

Add all the ingredients to a large pot, bring to a simmer, and cook for 25 minutes. Stir occasionally. If it gets too thick for your liking, add broth or tomato juice to thin. Adjust seasonings to taste.

Yield: 6 servings

Enchilada Sauce Variation

Follow the instructions in the main recipe (above), except omit the carrot and basil and add the following:

1 teaspoon ground cumin

1½ teaspoons chili powder

1 teaspoon crushed dry chile pepper (more to taste)

2 tablespoons (2 g) minced fresh cilantro

½ cup (75 g) minced red bell pepper

Yield: 6 servings

Pleasing Choco-Veggie Pot

This is a fairly simple but enjoyable single-pot meal pairing chocolate with several vegetables that are pleased to have its company. Vary the veggies for interesting nutritional and flavor combinations and consider adding cooked beans, nuts, tempeh, or other favorites. An important contribution toward overall health from vegetables is their insoluble fiber. As fiber passes through our digestive system, it absorbs water and expands, which helps promote regularity.

½ cup (80 g) chopped red onion

3 minced garlic cloves

2 cups (140 g) small whole cremini or button mushrooms

2 cups (240 g) diced zucchini

3 tablespoons (45 ml) olive oil

1 head Swiss chard, cut into ribbons

1½ cups (270 g) chopped tomatoes

2 tablespoons (8 g) chopped fresh oregano

2 tablespoons (28 ml) soy sauce or tamari

1 cup (260 g) sofrito or ajvar (see note)

½ cup (65 g) grated chocolate

½ cup (120 ml) mushroom or vegetable broth

¼ cup (60 ml) lemon juice

½ cup (30 g) chopped fresh Italian parsley

Begin by sautéing the onion, garlic, mushrooms, and zucchini in olive oil in a large pot over medium heat with a little salt. Add the swiss chard, tomatoes, and spices and cook for 2 minutes. Add the rest of the ingredients, except the lemon juice and parsley, and cook, stirring occasionally, for 20 minutes.

Add the parsley and lemon juice and cook for 10 minutes more. Season to taste.

Serve with toasted bread or seasoned rice or quinoa. This dish pairs well with wild rice or black rice.

NOTE: Sofrito is a sauce used in Italian, Portuguese, and Spanish cooking, often with olive oil, onions, and bell peppers. Ajvar is a type of relish found in Serbian and Greek cooking, made with red bell peppers and olive oil. You can make these items yourself or buy them premade.

Yield: 8 servings

Mouthwatering Chocolate Barbecue Sauce

This sauce is great with grilled vegetables, marinades, tofu, tempeh, mushrooms, eggplant, veggie burgers, or anything else your little heart desires! For some people, vegetables aren't done until a sauce has been added. This delicious barbecue sauce is for them! In addition, this healthy sauce doesn't contain the additives and preservatives found in many commercial brands.

2 cups (360 g) chopped seeded tomatoes

2 tablespoons (28 ml) tamari or soy sauce

1 teaspoon chili powder

½ teaspoon each ground cumin, paprika, black pepper

2 tablespoons (30 g) packed brown sugar or to taste

½ teaspoon garlic salt or smoked salt, or to taste

2 minced garlic cloves

2 teaspoons prepared mustard

1 tablespoon (15 ml) olive oil

¼ cup (40 g) chopped onion

1 teaspoon minced fresh hot chile pepper (Fresno is good.)

¼ teaspoon ground sage

1 to 2 tablespoons (15 to 28 ml) malt vinegar

½ cup (120 ml) broth or bouillon

2 ounces (55 g) grated unsweetened or bittersweet chocolate, or more to taste

Heat all of the ingredients except the chocolate and broth in a large saucepan over medium heat. Simmer for 30 minutes, adding the broth slowly as the tomatoes cook down.

Cool the mixture down and then purée in a blender. Return to the pot over medium heat and stir in the chocolate. Cook for an additional 10 minutes, adjusting seasonings to taste.

VARIATIONS: If the sauce seems too watery, add tomato paste or cornmeal, 1 teaspoon at a time, or just be mindful as you add the broth. You can also cut the tomatoes in half and slow roast them before making the sauce, which gives a different, richer flavor.

Yield: 8 servings

Cacao on the Brain: From Stroke Prevention to Cognitive Function

In 2013, the peer-reviewed journal *Nutrients* published a comprehensive article about the medical and nutritional history of chocolate. The authors covered many of the health benefits discussed in this book and said that we have come full circle with the original uses of cacao (in pre-Columbian Mesoamerica) and chocolate (in seventeenth- and eighteenth-century Europe) by eating it in a more whole form and less often as a confectionary. The current scientific interest in cacao, they summarize, recaptures what Carl Linnaeus meant in 1753 when he named the cacao plant *theobromine*, which translates to "food of the gods." In the eighteenth century, the scientific tools and medical knowledge Linnaeus had at his disposal were not what they are today.

The same is true, obviously, for the time when the Olmec, Maya, and Aztec civilizations used cacao extensively. Today's scientific evidence on cacao has the ability to show us the biologically active compounds that previously were only experienced. Historically, people have enjoyed it as if it was a gift from the gods, and now we know more about why that is true.

We know we have come a long way because the European Food Safety Agency in 2012 approved a health claim that cocoa flavanols contribute positively to normal blood flow. (To obtain the claimed effect, 200 milligrams of cocoa flavanols should be consumed daily. This amount could be provided by 2.5 grams of high-flavanol cocoa powder or 10 grams of high-flavanol dark chocolate.) More than 250 years after Linnaeus's description, we have a strong, evidence-based health claim on the benefits of cacao—Full circle indeed.

Cacao has a plethora of positive effects on the brain and cognitive function, including increased cerebral blood flow and concentration, mood improvement, reduced mental fatigue, and reduced risk of dementia, stroke, and Alzheimer's disease. Also, simply, it provides enjoyment. As one of the most craved foods in the world, chocolate has a near symbiotic relationship with our brain. Read on for a discussion of what we know about how cacao affects the brain both physiologically and psychologically.

Cacao Keeps the Blood Flowing to the Brain

Stroke, defined as a rapid loss of blood to the brain because of a blockage or hemorrhage, is a leading cause of disability in the United States and the fourth leading cause of death. Risk factors include some of the disorders we've previously discussed: high blood pressure, high cholesterol, and diabetes (and old age, but there's nothing we can do about that!).

Those who consume cacao regularly may have a lower risk of stroke because cacao's flavonoids increase blood flow. One 2012 study followed 37,103 Swedish men for 10.2 years and found that high chocolate consumption was associated with reduced risk of stroke. When researchers compared the group that ate the most chocolate, about 60 grams per week, with those who ate no chocolate, the protective benefits were even more pronounced.

The same authors then did what's called a meta-analysis, calculating data from five other similar studies. What they found corroborated with their original findings: Those who ate chocolate regularly were less likely to have a stroke. The mechanism is no doubt related to flavonoids' ability to help increase blood flow in the middle cerebral artery. Additionally, cacao's ability to lower blood pressure, cholesterol, and type 2 diabetes risk indirectly protects against stroke.

Cacao: A Great Source of Vitamin Pleasure

Flavonoids are the category of polyphenols that includes flavanols, flavan-3-ols, anthocyanins, proanthocyanidins, catechin, epicatechin, flavonols, and flavones. Upon discovery in the 1930s, flavonoids were called vitamin P. This terminology didn't last, because flavonoids technically are not a vitamin.

Coincidentally, though, in modern-day vernacular vitamin P stands for, among other things, vitamin pleasure. This term is used when discussing the fact that people who are happier and enjoy their food more have fewer chronic diseases than would be predicted by their diet. Being happy when you eat translates into living a healthier life, according to some studies. Doesn't that make you happy? This is also sometimes called the French paradox, because the French regularly consume foods high in cholesterol and saturated fat, but do not have the associated rates of disease one would expect. One explanation is that the French take more time to eat their meals and enjoy them. Another reason is their high consumption of fruits, vegetables, and wine, which contain polyphenols like flavonoids, the original vitamin P! Eating cacao is a pleasurable experience, and it is high in polyphenols: both vitamin P and vitamin pleasure together at last.

Cognitive Cacao

Increased blood flow to the brain undoubtedly impacts other cerebral functions. The benefits of cacao include positive neurochemical effects that may slow degenerative diseases of the brain and improve cognition.

Alzheimer's disease. Alzheimer's is an irreversible brain disease in which memory and the ability to perform basic skills are lost. It is the leading cause of dementia, a condition that involves the deterioration of decision making and reasoning parts of the brain. The cause of Alzheimer's is not fully understood, but some researchers hypothesize that it could be considered type 3 diabetes. An independent risk factor for Alzheimer's is metabolic syndrome, same as it is for type 2 diabetes, which is one reason to believe the conditions are related. According to a 2012 paper in *Rejuvenation Research*, an association between metabolic syndrome and gene encoding related to insulin signaling affects the brain. The authors believe new knowledge in molecular biology and epigenetics will soon lead to earlier diagnoses of dementia.

There are a lot of parallels between the understanding of Alzheimer's now and heart disease fifty years ago. At that time, doctors and researchers thought that the heart simply stopped working with the onset of old age. Now we know that the development of the plaque that leads to heart disease begins decades before a heart attack happens, and we can control some factors to limit the onset of disease.

There may be similar findings for Alzheimer's and dementia in the future. Right now, some research says cacao can delay the onset of Alzheimer's and cognitive disorders. In 2013, the journal *Neurology* published a study done at Brigham and Women's Hospital, a Harvard-affiliated research hospital, which involved sixty people with an average age of seventy-three. Half the group drank high-flavanol cocoa and the other half low-flavanol cocoa for thirty days. Researchers examined participants' memory and thinking skills at the beginning and end of the study, using ultrasound to perform neurovascular coupling tests, which look at the blood flow response to brain activity. The results were intriguing. Those with impaired blood flow response showed statistically significant improvement after thirty days of consuming flavanol-rich cocoa. And what about the thinking tests? Time taken to complete the tests decreased by 30 percent, showing evidence for reduced mental fatigue from cacao consumption. Lastly, the investigators performed brain MRIs and found that those with limited neurovascular coupling had the most damaged white matter. They concluded that there is a strong correlation between regular cocoa consumption and cognitive function.

Cacao's Stimulus Package

Cacao contains small amounts of the stimulant methylxanthine in the form of caffeine and theobromine. Even though the amount of these stimulants is very low compared to coffee or tea, they are pharmacologically active compounds and may partly explain the feel-good nature of chocolate.

Some creative researchers have taken a look at this by serving sixty-four participants a cocoa drink that also included taking a pill. Half of the pills had the equivalent caffeine and theobromine of 50 grams of chocolate, and the other half were placebos. The result was highly significant: Those who received the pills with the stimulants were much more likely to say they enjoyed the drink. And remember, the caffeine content was equivalent to 50 grams of dark chocolate, which is only 19 milligrams. This is a very small amount of caffeine as compared to the amount in a cup of coffee (95 milligrams), but apparently is significant enough in this scenario. The researchers concluded that part of the positive effects of consuming cacao products are related to the stimulants caffeine and theobromine.

Stress and Anxiety: Chocolate to the Rescue

Stress is a physiological response that can negatively impact our cardiovascular system if not dealt with appropriately. Our bodies have a fight-or-flight mechanism to enable us to ward off danger. But in today's modern world, too many people are in a constant state of stress, as if every day is dangerous with no respite. Most of us have never developed healthy coping strategies, and this chronic stress wreaks havoc on our physiological system.

Stress can also indirectly affect our health by leading to poor decisions such as overeating or using unhealthy foods as coping mechanisms. How we deal with stress is a very important component of overall well-being, and chocolate, long thought of as a guilty pleasure, can be a positive contribution to stress management.

Researchers in a 2009 clinical study in Switzerland fed thirty participants 40 grams of dark chocolate daily for two weeks to analyze the metabolic impact of dark chocolate. Not everyone had significant results, but one important group did: those with high levels of anxiety. Regular chocolate consumption reduced the metabolic markers related to anxiety, such as urine levels of the stress hormone cortisol. The authors concluded that this was strong evidence for the daily consumption of dark chocolate.

Socialized Chocolate Love Is Still Chocolate Love

The previously mentioned research lends evidence to the argument that bioactive compounds in cacao affect our brain in positive ways. However, some scientists just argue that cacao has unique orosensory properties, which is just a fancy way to say it tastes good, we like to eat it, and that makes us happy.

This isn't necessarily a bad thing. A food doesn't have to have proven biochemical components to create positive outcomes. That can happen because you simply have a pleasurable experience when you eat it. Remember vitamin pleasure? Some researchers have looked at this. When American and Spanish women were asked open-ended questions about food cravings, there was a tenfold difference in preference for chocolate. American women are more likely to eat and enjoy chocolate so are therefore more likely to have cravings for it.

Think about it this way: Cocoa butter crystallizes just below body temperature. It melts in your mouth with a sensation totally unique to cacao. This creates a wonderful mouthfeel (a real scientific term!) that releases positive endorphins because it feels good, not necessarily because of the components in chocolate.

Excitement over chocolate is, for many people, a socialized, learned behavior. If we look at the status that chocolate has, it's no wonder we have such strong feelings about it. Holidays such as Easter, Day of the Dead, Valentine's Day, Christmas, Hanukkah, and Diwali, to name a few, often involve chocolate. Although the research continues to trickle in with the scientific reasons for why we crave and enjoy cacao products, keep eating it for whichever reasons make you happy.

Putting It into Practice

- The benefits of cacao work best in cohort with a plant-based whole-foods approach. This is true not only for your health, but for your taste buds. Most of us are used to the incredible sweetness of refined sugars; give these up for two weeks and your taste buds will rejoice! Fruits will taste sweeter and you'll experience the subtle tastes in foods such as cacao and chocolate that you never knew were possible. Try the same approach by reducing the amount of salt in your diet and watch your taste buds expand.

- Our brains don't like change; which is why starting an exercise program or taking personal risks is so difficult. When you eat new foods, your immediate reaction may be dislike. But do you really feel this way, or is it your brain's response to change? Don't let it fool you! Keep trying new foods until they aren't new anymore, and you may be surprised at what you actually like and enjoy.

- We've learned in this chapter that some of the beneficial mental aspects of cacao and chocolate are learned. Some may view this as a negative, but I think it's a positive because you can relearn and reassociate experiences that lead to increased mental well-being. Preparing meals is a personal example of mine. I love it and look forward to it, so I am excited when it is dinnertime. What new, healthy behaviors can you reassociate with a positive mental attitude?

- The brain needs active stimulation in addition to a healthy diet. Like our heart, it needs to work out every day by doing stimulating activities. I think creative cooking counts, as it is both an art and a science. So work your brain out in more ways than one by cooking up some of our healthy cacao recipes.

CHAPTER FIVE

Recipes at a Glance

Croque Chocolat with Sun-Dried Tomato Pesto, Roasted Eggplant, and Arugula

Chocolate melted onto a sandwich will become an addiction whether it is this, PB&J, a vegetarian Reuben, or a BLT!! Eggplant has a wonderful texture that makes it an ideal sandwich ingredient. And like other vegetables, it's nutrient dense and low in calories. Sun-dried tomatoes are also a great source of the minerals iron, magnesium, and potassium.

1 eggplant, in ¼-inch (6 mm) slices

4 to 5 tablespoons (60 to 75 ml) olive oil, divided

1 to 1½ teaspoons salt, divided

4 minced garlic cloves, divided

¼ teaspoon black pepper

2 tablespoons (28 ml) + 2 teaspoons balsamic vinegar, divided

1 cup (55 g) sun-dried tomatoes

2 tablespoons (8 g) minced fresh parsley

¼ cup (40 g) chopped red onion

½ cup (20 g) basil leaves

⅓ cup (33 g) pitted kalamata olives

1 tablespoon (15 ml) lemon juice

¼ cup (35 g) toasted pine nuts or other preferred nut or seed

Panini or crusty French bread slices for 4 sandwiches

2 tablespoons (30 g) Dijon mustard mixed with 2 teaspoons raw cacao powder

4 ounces (115 g) dark chocolate, shaved or sliced very thin

1 to 2 cups (20 to 40 g) arugula

1 teaspoon capers

Preheat the oven to 400°F (200°C, gas mark 6).

Place the eggplant slices on a greased baking pan in a single layer. Brush with 1 tablespoon (15 ml) oil, sprinkle with ¼ to ½ teaspoon salt, 1 minced garlic clove, and the pepper. Drizzle 2 teaspoons balsamic vinegar on top and bake for 25 minutes. Remove from the oven.

Purée the rest of the balsamic vinegar, salt, and garlic with the tomatoes, parsley, onion, basil, olives, lemon juice, and nuts. Set aside.

Toast the bread slices for 5 minutes in the oven and remove. Switch the oven to broil. Spread mustard on each slice of bread, followed by the pesto, eggplant, and chocolate. Place on a large baking sheet and broil for 1 minute. Remove from the oven. Add the arugula and capers to 4 of the slices and then pair these with the other 4 to make sandwiches.

Yield: 4 servings

Cocoa-Potato Tacos

Here's what to do with your leftover mashed potatoes! And One-Hour Mole (page 50) is made for this sort of thing. Forget about potatoes being a plain starch; they are also a source of iron, potassium, vitamin C, and even protein. You can always brighten this dish up by using sweet, purple, or gold potatoes. Corn tortillas are no nutritional slouch either. They contain significantly more calcium than corn because of how they are made (with limewater).

½ teaspoon salt

1 teaspoon chili powder

1 tablespoon (5 g) cocoa powder

2 teaspoons olive or canola oil

2 teaspoons lime juice

2 cups (450 g) cooked mashed potatoes

2 minced garlic cloves

½ cup (80 g) sliced onions

2 tablespoons (8 g) grated bittersweet chocolate (more to taste)

2 to 3 tablespoons (2 to 3 g) minced fresh cilantro

8 to 10 corn tortillas

Olive oil, for brushing and sautéing

Lime wedges, for serving

Stir the salt, chili powder, cocoa powder, oil, and lime juice into the mashed potatoes in a medium mixing bowl (or magical bowler hat). Set aside.

Sauté the garlic and onions in a little oil in a large skillet over medium-high heat for 2 minutes. Add the mashed potatoes, lower the heat to medium, and cook, flipping until browned in places (this will take around 4 minutes per "side"). Scoop into the tortillas (about ⅓ cup [85 g] per tortilla), sprinkle with grated chocolate, cilantro, a little lime juice, and chile sauce and fold over. Cook in very light oil in a skillet over medium heat, turning once, until crispy on both sides (around 2 to 3 minutes per side). Or alternately brush with oil and bake at 400°F (200°C, gas mark 6), turning once, for 7 to 10 minutes or until the shells are browned. You can also not bother with the oil if you don't wish to.

SUGGESTIONS: The One-Hour Mole (page 50) or the Enchilada Sauce variation of the Chocolate Marinara (page 113) go very well with these tacos, as does salsa or avocado. For a spicy kick, add 2 tablespoons (11 g) chopped or sliced jalapeños to the sauté.

Yield: 8 servings

Chocolate-Carrot Pie

Here you get to use up some of that huge bag of carrots from the farm share you've been juicing! Their natural sweetness is a perfect fit with chocolate. Most likely you are familiar with orange carrots, but did you know there are purple, white, and even red carrots? Each color is high in a different phytochemical, so go ahead and "eat your colors" when it comes to carrots, too.

1 unbaked Do-It-Yourself Cocoa Piecrust (page 172)

1½ cups (165 g) grated carrots

1 cup (132 g) melted bittersweet chocolate

½ cup (100 g) sugar

½ cup (80 g) rice, (56 g) almond, or (68 g) sorghum flour

1 tablespoon (8 g) cornstarch or tapioca starch

½ teaspoon salt (more to taste)

1 teaspoon ground cinnamon

½ teaspoon grated nutmeg

¼ teaspoon ground cloves

½ teaspoon ground ginger

Preheat the oven to 425°F (220°C, gas mark 7).

Press the piecrust into a 9-inch (23 cm) pie dish. For an interesting variation, add ground pecans or coconut at this time by pressing gently into the crust.

Mix the rest of the ingredients in a large bowl or, for a smoother texture, in a blender. Pour into the pie shell. Bake for 15 minutes and then lower the heat to 375°F (190°C, gas mark 5) and bake for another 25 minutes. Serve or cool and refrigerate.

SUGGESTIONS: Serve with Basic Double Chocolate Sauce (page 164) and Cocoa-Coconut Cream (page 191), which you can use to cover the entire pie for a cream pie. In this case, sprinkle the pie with toasted coconut after spreading the cream on top.

Yield: 8 servings

Chocolaty Bindi Masala

This easy Indian dish is made even more mouthwatering with a chocolate addition. It teaches that okra a lesson! Indian spices have long been recognized for their medicine-like qualities. And Western science is finally catching up. Turmeric, one of the main ingredients in curry powder, contains the powerful anti-inflammatory curcumin. It may help prevent cancer and in the future may even be used to treat disease.

½ cup (80 g) chopped red onion

2 minced garlic cloves

½ teaspoon mustard seeds

2 tablespoons (28 ml) olive oil

3 cups (300 g) sliced okra

2 teaspoons garam masala

1 teaspoon curry powder

2 minced hot chile peppers (optional)

2 cups (360 g) diced tomatoes

1 cup (150 g) diced sweet or bell peppers

½ cup (65 g) grated bittersweet chocolate

¼ cup (64 g) tamarind purée

2 tablespoons (28 ml) lime juice

Salt and white pepper, to taste

1 cup (235 ml) coconut milk or vegetable broth

2 tablespoons (2 g) minced fresh cilantro

Sauté the onion, garlic, and mustard seeds in the oil in a large pot over medium heat. Add the okra, spices, and chiles and cook for a few minutes. Add the rest of the ingredients except the coconut milk and cilantro and simmer for 15 minutes. Add the cilantro and coconut milk and cook for another 10 minutes, adding more spice if needed.

Serve this dish with rice, raita, and naan.

Yield: 6 servings

Cinnamon-Cashew Bake

This is an unusual and delicious dish to warm you up! Cinnamon and cashews go well with chocolate in savory as well as sweet dishes! Cashews are lower in fat than most nuts (Cashews aren't really nuts, they're seeds—that's why.), and the majority of their fat is the unsaturated, heart-healthy kind. In addition, much of it is the fatty acid oleic acid, the same beneficial fat found in olive oil.

2 tablespoons (10 g) cocoa powder

1½ cups (143 g) ground cashews, divided

2 to 3 tablespoons (28 to 45 ml) olive oil, divided

1½ teaspoons ground cinnamon, divided

¼ cup (25 g) chopped scallions

2 cups (496 g) tofu, (140 g) mushroom, or (332 g) tempeh, cut into 2- × 2-inch (5 × 5 cm) squares

1 cup (130 g) diced carrots

1 cup (82 g) diced eggplant

½ cup (60 g) diced celery

1 cup (150 g) diced red, yellow, and/or green bell peppers

1 cup (160 g) diced onions

2 minced garlic cloves

⅓ cup (44 g) melted chocolate

1 teaspoon minced lemongrass

1 teaspoon curry powder

2 tablespoons (28 ml) lime or lemon juice

2 tablespoons (28 ml) balsamic vinegar

Soy sauce or tamari, to taste

Salt and black pepper, to taste

Preheat the oven to 400°F (200°C, gas mark 6).

Combine all the ingredients in a large bowl except the cocoa powder, ½ cup (48 g) cashews, 1 teaspoon oil, ½ teaspoon cinnamon, and the scallions. Place the mixture in an 8- × 11-inch (20 × 28 cm) greased casserole dish. Sprinkle with the reserved ingredients and bake for 40 minutes. Serve with seasoned rice, chutney, and chile sauce.

Yield: 8 servings

Huitlacoche Empanadas

If you haven't had huitlacoche (or cuitlacoche), you're missing out. In the United States, it gets the unflattering name of "corn smut" because it is a fungus that grows in corn husks. American farmers consider it a blight. In Mexico, it is considered a delicacy and can even be expensive! It is a natural fit with chocolate with its mild, earthy, trufflelike taste. Canned, jarred, or fresh works for this recipe.

1 cup (70 g) chopped huitlacoche (Another mushroom can be substituted.)

¼ cup (40 g) minced onion

⅓ cup (43 g) grated bittersweet, dark, or unsweetened chocolate

2 tablespoons (28 ml) chipotle sauce

¼ cup sweet corn, (39 g) fresh, (41 g) frozen, or (53 g) canned

½ teaspoon each ground cumin and chili powder

¼ cup (4 g) chopped fresh cilantro

1 teaspoon lime juice or cider vinegar

1 teaspoon minced fresh oregano

Salt and black pepper, to taste

1 to 2 tablespoons (15 to 28 ml) olive oil

1 batch of Do-It-Yourself Cocoa Piecrust (page 172), sugar omitted, and ½ teaspoon garlic powder and 1 teaspoon baking powder added

Preheat the oven to 425°F (220°C, gas mark 7).

In a large bowl, combine all the ingredients except the oil and piecrust. Set aside.

Roll out twelve to sixteen 4-inch (10 cm) rounds of piecrust on a lightly floured board, to a ⅛- to ¼-inch (3 to 6 mm) thickness. Place 2 tablespoons (28 g) of the mixture in the middle of the round, slightly to one side. Fold over to make little turnovers and crimp the edges by folding about ¼ inch (6 mm) of the bottom edge over the top edge. You can use your fingers, a pastry wheel, or a fork to cinch the seam, making decorative patterns while doing so.

Baste lightly with the oil for a crispier result or skip this step for softer empanadas. Bake on a lightly greased baking sheet for 20 to 25 minutes or until browned. Serve with salsa or mole.

Yield: 12 to 16 empanadas

Chocolate Jamaica

With this recipe, you can familiarize yourself with using hibiscus. Hibiscus contains the flavonoid anthocyanin that is also found in blueberries, cherries, and acai berries. This beverage is vaguely tea-like. Dried hibiscus (*jamaica* in Spanish) can be found in a Mexican or Caribbean grocery store or often in a large super-market, usually by the tamarind pods.

8 cups (1.9 L) water

1 cinnamon stick, crushed

½ cup (100 g) sugar, or to taste

1 cup (84 g) dried hibiscus flowers

¼ cup (60 ml) lemon or lime juice

½ cup (150 g) Homemade Chocolate Syrup (page 139)

Bring the water, cinnamon, and sugar to a boil in a large pot. Add the hibiscus flowers. Remove from the heat, add the lime juice, and steep for half an hour. Strain and cool. Add to glasses over ice and stir 2 tablespoons (38 g) of chocolate syrup, or to taste, into each glass.

VARIATIONS:

• You can use fruit juice for 2 to 4 cups (475 to 950 ml) of the liquid and omit the sugar altogether!

• Instead of the Homemade Chocolate Syrup, bring ½ cup (40 g) cocoa powder to a boil with the water and add a bit more sugar.

Yield: 8 servings

Bloody Cocoa Mary

I couldn't resist one of these cocktails, which is not for the faint-hearted! Horseradish and chocolate remain an unexplored pairing in society, I daresay. Sure, vodka is not exactly a health food. But the benefits of moderate alcohol consumption are well established, and this is a fun, occasional way to get some alcohol and cacao together. If you don't drink alcohol, see the variations below.

2 tablespoons (10 g) cocoa powder

2 cups (475 ml) vegetable juice (tomato heavy)

2 tablespoons (28 ml) lemon juice

1 tablespoon (3 g) minced sun-dried tomatoes

1 teaspoon balsamic vinegar

1 teaspoon tamari

1 teaspoon grated horseradish

1 teaspoon grated ginger

Black pepper, to taste

4 to 6 ounces (120 to 175 g) vodka

For garnish: shaved chocolate ribbons, pickled asparagus, olives, carrot sticks, lemon peel

Blend the cocoa powder through black pepper in a blender. Pour vodka into 2 glasses over ice and then add the juice mixture. Stir.

Add a pickled asparagus spear, olives, carrot, and lemon peel and garnish with shaved chocolate.

VARIATION: If you want to avoid alcohol, some fun things to use instead of vodka include cucumber juice, aloe juice, cactus juice, or kombucha! Each of these will add its own fabulous flavor and nutritional benefits to this drink, and you won't have to worry about being naughty!

Yield: 2 servings

Bump Up Your Day the Miso (Soup) Way

Miso and cacao are another natural fit. Play around with this rich and luxurious combination. There's reason to believe that the fermentation process of miso increases the amount of antioxidants available from the soybean, making this soup a phytochemical powerhouse.

5 cups (1.2 L) broth, vegetable or mushroom, or water with 1 or 2 bouillon cubes

⅓ to ½ cup (32 to 48 g) raw cacao powder

1 teaspoon minced chile pepper

1 teaspoon minced or grated ginger

1 minced garlic clove

¼ cup (64 g) miso paste (or less for a less salty taste)

8 ounces (225 g) tofu, cut into small cubes

½ cup (50 g) sliced scallions

1 or 2 tablespoons agave nectar (20 or 40 g) or (13 or 26 g) coconut sugar (optional)

Lemon wedges

Bring the broth, cacao powder, chile, ginger, and garlic to a simmer in a large pot. Cook for 10 minutes, stirring occasionally. Stir in the miso, combining well. Add the tofu and scallions and simmer for 3 or 4 more minutes. Add the optional sweetener. Remove from the heat. Sprinkle with lemon juice, if desired.

Yield: 4 servings

Avocado-Cocoa Mousse with Persian Spiced Cream

The Persian spice mix *panch phoran* typically contains ajwain (lovage seed), kalonji (nigella seed), fenugreek, fennel seed, mustard seed, and sometimes cumin. If you can't find it, you can make your own by mixing equal portions of the spices and seeds. This dish is a fun way to sneak in iron, protein, and fiber in the form of cannellini beans.

16 ounces (455 g) lasagna noodles, cooked

FOR THE MOUSSE:

3 avocados, pitted and peeled

2 tablespoons (28 ml) lemon juice

⅓ cup (80 g) coconut cream or (60 g) cooked mashed cannellini beans

Salt, to taste

⅓ cup (27 g) cocoa powder (unsweetened, raw, or other)

2 tablespoons (28 ml) olive oil

FOR THE CREAM:

1 tablespoon (7 g) panch phoran Persian spice blend

1 cup (179 g) cooked mashed cannellini beans or 1 cup (240 g) coconut cream or a combination

Salt and white pepper, to taste

1 tablespoon (15 ml) lemon juice

2 tablespoons (28 ml) olive oil (or use half truffle oil)

2 garlic cloves

¼ cup (24 g) raw cacao powder

FOR THE MUSHROOMS:

1 cup (70 g) mixed wild mushrooms, chopped

1 tablespoon (10 g) minced onion

1 garlic clove, minced

2 teaspoons olive oil

½ teaspoon minced fresh thyme

1 teaspoon balsamic vinegar (or Chocolate Balsamic Reduction [page 107], even better)

Salt and black pepper, to taste

1 ounce (28 g) dark chocolate

TO MAKE THE MOUSSE: Blend the avocado with the other ingredients until smooth and creamy, either in a food processor or by hand in a bowl. Adjust seasonings to taste and chill before serving.

TO MAKE THE CREAM: Toast the panch phoran for 2 minutes in a dry pan over medium heat. Then blend with the other ingredients in a food processor until smooth and adjust seasonings to taste.

TO MAKE THE MUSHROOMS: Sauté the mushrooms with the onion and garlic in the oil for 1 minute in a medium skillet over medium heat, add the rest of the ingredients, and sauté for 2 more minutes. Remove from the heat.

To compose the dish, place a scoop of mousse in a glass, add a generous spoonful of the mushrooms slightly to the side, and then a dollop of the cream on the middle. Grate some of the dark chocolate on top.

Yield: 6 servings

Homemade Chocolate Syrup

This is a great syrup that can be added to a variety of drinks. When you make it at home, you can control the quality and quantity of the ingredients. Using high-quality cocoa and unrefined sugars makes this a more nutritious choice than any chocolate syrup you can buy.

1 cup (235 ml) water

½ to 1 cup (100 to 200 g) unrefined sugar, or to taste

1 cup (80 g) cocoa powder

2 tablespoons (40 g) agave nectar or maple syrup

Pinch salt

1 teaspoon vanilla

Combine the water, sugar, cocoa powder, agave, and salt in a heavy medium-size saucepan and bring to a simmer. Cook for about 10 minutes or until thickened, stirring on occasion. Add the vanilla, remove from the heat, and allow to cool.

VARIATION: Use 1½ cups (355 ml) fruit juice instead of the sugar and water and cook for 15 to 20 minutes to thicken a bit. Use cherry, pomegranate, blackberry, or blueberry juice, for example.

Yield: 8 servings

Triple Chocolate Bruschetta

For those of you who enjoy chocolate every way it comes, here's a clever invention! The sweet acidity of heirloom tomatoes both cuts through and complements the chocolate highlights. And while the combination is pleasing to your tongue, the two work together nutritionally because the fatty acids from the cacao aid the absorption of the phytochemical lycopene in the tomatoes.

¼ cup (43 g) kalamata olives, pitted and chopped

¼ cup (25 g) shaved chocolate

½ cup (90 g) chopped, drained heirloom tomatoes

¼ cup (45 g) chopped roasted red bell pepper

1 tablespoon (10 g) minced red onion

1 minced garlic clove, or to taste

1 tablespoon (3 g) minced fresh basil

1 to 2 teaspoons olive oil

2 teaspoons capers

1 teaspoon balsamic vinegar or Chocolate Balsamic Reduction (page 107)

Salt and freshly ground black pepper, to taste

½ cup (66 g) melted bittersweet chocolate blended with 1 teaspoon tomato sauce

12 to 16 toasted baguette slices

In a large bowl, gently mix together the olives through the salt and pepper. Set aside.

Coat one end of each baguette slice in a bit of the melted chocolate and cool on wax paper. When set, add a spoonful of the tomato topping on each and serve. It's delicious!

Yield: 6 servings

Super Snack: Cacao to Fuel Your Physical Activity

In 1953, Nepalese Sherpa Tenzing Norgay and New Zealand mountaineer Edmund Hillary were attempting to scale the world's highest peak, Mount Everest, known locally as Chomolungma. The first expeditions had taken place more than 30 years earlier without anyone officially reaching the summit. Mount Everest had already taken at least two lives. The situation was dire for Norgay and Hillary in May of that year; they spent two days in a tent at nearly 26,000-foot elevation waiting for the weather to clear to attempt the summit. It eventually cleared enough, and the two did what no one had ever done before them: They stood on the top of the tallest mountain in the world. They stayed there for only fifteen minutes, and Hillary left a cross as an offering on the top before they made the equally dangerous descent. And what about Norgay? He left pieces of chocolate.

I like to imagine Norgay and Hillary sitting in their tent near the top of the world, passing time and sharing chocolate awaiting the unknown. It's no surprise they had chocolate with them. Even before knowing what we know now about cacao, it was a popular food for mountaineers, explorers, and soldiers all over the world. In pre-Columbian times, cacao was eaten regularly by some folks with pretty intense physical requirements: Aztec warriors. Back then, in those tropical climates, they consumed a frothy drink made from cacao, not chocolate bars like the ones Norgay and Hillary were eating. They did not have to worry about melting! They believed that cacao imparted strength and inspiration straight from Quetzalcoatl. Whatever the form, cacao is a great companion of physical exertion from mountaineers and Aztec warriors to recreational runners and weekend warriors.

Today cacao and chocolate are still popular foods for athletes during workouts and in recovery. Cacao's benefits are outstanding: It is calorically and nutrient dense, it supplies small amounts of stimulation from theobromine and caffeine that may help prolong physical activity, and it may improve the widening of blood vessels, which brings more oxygen to your muscles. Plus, it's delicious. I've been in long races and on wilderness trips lasting many weeks where chocolate hits the spot. Once I was bike touring through a remote mountainous region of Montana, riding more than 130 miles day for many days in a row. There were very few people or stores around, and I had to carefully choose what foods I would carry. After an arduous day of physical exertion and making dinner, enjoying the solitude, and taking in my surroundings, a small piece of dark chocolate was the perfect way to end the day.

Cacao: The Whole-Food, Plant-Based Way to Get the Energy You Need

One surprising issue that comes up when I work with athletes is that they are simply not consuming enough calories to fuel their workouts. Some athletes, even recreational ones, can have caloric demands of upwards of 8,000 calories a day! Too often athletes are instructed to get their calories any way they can, with little concern about the healthiness of the food they are eating. It is a myth that because athletes are fit they do not need to be concerned about healthy eating or chronic disease risk. By getting exercise, you reduce your risk, but you still have to be mindful of other risk factors such as poor diet, high cholesterol, and family history. Your diet and lifestyle still greatly affect your overall health, even if you are physically active. Cacao can both supply the energy you need now and help prevent chronic disease in the future.

The Nutritional Makeup of Cacao Beans Is Beneficial for Physical Activity

Many of the foods touted for their high phytochemical content, such as tea, berries, and wine, are not calorically dense. Cacao holds a unique position as a phytochemically rich, calorically dense food that can play a key role in getting the energy you need for your physical activity, in a health-promoting way. The majority of calories in cacao come from fat, but cacao also contains carbohydrate and protein—nutrients required for physical activity. One ounce (28 g) of cacao beans, nibs, or powder contains roughly 160 calories (exact numbers will vary; be sure to check the labels). And cocoa powder, which is much lower in fat because the cocoa butter has been removed, is still a good source of the beneficial components of cacao. It's also easy to make hot chocolate with, a delicious recovery drink, for those cold-weather training days.

Cacao, of course, is more than calories and energy. The nutrients it contains, in particular magnesium and iron, do more than help you meet your recommended daily intake; they can actually improve physical performance. Here's how.

Magnesium. Magnesium is a cofactor in more than 300 enzyme reactions in the body from muscle and nerve function to protein synthesis. It is part of the structural development of bone and is involved with the synthesis of DNA and RNA.

One study on magnesium found that it has a significant role in muscle development and strength-training performance, yet intake of magnesium for athletes can often be below recommended levels. This same study found that depleted magnesium levels reduced the strength ability of trained athletes on a variety of performance tests. The mechanisms responsible, according to the study, are related to the role of magnesium in energetic metabolism and muscle contraction and relaxation.

Another study found that reduced magnesium intake resulted in increased energy needs and adversely affected cardiovascular function during moderate exercise. Cacao is an excellent source of magnesium: One ounce (28 g) contains nearly 25 percent of the Daily Value, more than a serving of almonds or spinach, both of which are great sources of magnesium. Cacao is a terrific way to get the recommended amount of this crucial mineral while training and exercising because you also get the beneficial antioxidants we'll learn more about below.

Iron. The increased risk of iron-deficiency anemia in athletes is well established, especially for premenopausal women. Iron is a part of hemoglobin that carries oxygen and energy through the blood. It is also contained in ferritin complexes in every single cell. Iron deficiency is one of the most common nutrient deficiencies in the world, and one of the major symptoms is fatigue—the enemy of well-intentioned physically active people everywhere. Cacao contains significant amounts of iron that can be beneficial to athletes before, during, and after workouts. An important concern with iron is absorption; when smaller amounts at a time are consumed, as is the case with cacao, absorption increases. Therefore, it is advantageous to get your iron from a variety of sources throughout the day.

How Stimulating: The Caffeine and Theobromine Content of Cacao

Cacao contains small but significant amounts of the stimulants caffeine and theobromine. Caffeine is a natural insecticide for plants. Most people who already consume caffeine in the form of coffee, tea, or energy drinks won't notice the added stimulation from cacao. For others, a piece of dark chocolate late in the afternoon is enough to keep them up at night! Like other components of cacao, the darker the chocolate, the more caffeine and theobromine you are consuming. An important consideration is this: The higher the cacao content of what you are eating, the less likely you are to overeat because of the strong taste of cacao. An entire 3.5-ounce (100 g) dark chocolate bar can contain about 80 milligrams of caffeine, about as much as in 6 ounces (175 ml) of coffee—a small amount by today's standards. One ounce (28 g) then only has about 22 milligrams, which is less than the amount in 3 ounces (90 ml) of green tea.

Theobromine is an alkaloid and a stimulant to the central nervous system that is unique to cacao, tea leaves, and the kola nut. It is in the methylxanthine class of compounds, like caffeine, but its effect is significantly milder. It functions biologically as a vasodilator, a mild diuretic, and a heart stimulant, and research continues to explore its effect on exercise and other functions.

There is fairly extensive research that caffeine is useful for athletes competing in sprints, endurance exercises, and strength training. Too much caffeine, however, can lead to irritability, jitteriness, anxiety, nausea, muscle spasms, and even death. The amount of caffeine and theobromine in cacao is significant enough to trigger physiological responses that may be beneficial to athletes, with little risk of overconsumption.

Cacao: Improved Blood Flow for Athletes, Legally

Blood vessels relax and widen in a process known as vasodilation. With wider blood vessels, more oxygen-rich blood flows through the body and reaches muscles sooner. With more oxygen and improved oxygen delivery, muscles are able to work at high intensity for longer periods of time. Increased blood flow also helps to dissipate the heat created during physical activity.

Elite athletes have long tried to find ways to increase vasodilation, including through illegal substances. But you don't have to cheat to widen your blood vessels. Consuming beets and beet juice is showing promising results and is very popular with athletes right now. Beets, and to a lesser extent spinach and carrots, increase blood flow because of their nitrate content. Beets supply naturally occurring, nonsynthetic nitrates that are converted to nitric oxide, which increases vasodilation. (See our Rich Borscht with Cacao Accent on page 75 to get the benefits of cacao and beets together!)

According to a Harvard Medical School study, cacao is associated with increased blood flow because of the positive effect flavanols have on this nitric oxide system. The theobromine in cacao also increases vasodilation. What we do know about cacao and vasodilation is that the cardiovascular benefits can be applied to physical activity, making it useful before, during, and after workouts. Meanwhile, we'll wait for the more specific research about how similarly beneficial it is to beets. The future is promising.

Cacao: Recover Faster with Phytochemicals

Those same powerful phytochemicals that help prevent chronic disease may help improve physical performance as well. The flavanols and other phytochemicals found in cacao repair damaged cells and reduce free radicals, which is especially beneficial for athletes who are constantly building and repairing muscles and creating oxidative stress. One of the main benefits cited by athletes who eat a plant-based diet, such as Scott Jurek and Rich Roll, is their ability to recover faster after their workouts, which is well-established by significant research.

The oxidative stress from training damages mitochondrial DNA, cells, and tissues and creates free radicals—processes we usually want to reduce. So what is an athlete to do? The answer is to eat phytochemical-rich foods such as cacao, fruits, and vegetables in large amounts to reduce postworkout oxidative stress, repair our cells, minimize free radicals, and reduce recovery time. The faster you can recover after a hard exertion, say running 100 miles in under 24 hours like Scott Jurek does, the sooner you can do your next workout. The more workouts you do, the fitter you will become. Faster recovery leads to better fitness faster, and cacao can have a crucial role in this process, no matter your current fitness level or athletic goals.

Putting It into Practice

- Athletes often want to tough it out and deny themselves tasty food. With cacao, you can have both: taste and performance enhancement.

- One of the simplest ways to incorporate cacao into your diet plan is in smoothies. A simple formula to start with is 1 cup (235 ml) nondairy milk, 1 banana, 1 cup (225 g) frozen fruit, 1 tablespoon (16 g) nut butter, and 1 tablespoon (6 g) raw cacao powder. Combine in a blender. Any smoothie can benefit from the addition of cacao, so try adding it to your own!

- Chocolate has a low melting point, but cacao nibs do not. Add them to your trail mix when you go on hikes or as snacks for a long day and you don't have to worry about melting.

- For physical activity that lasts many hours, chocolate can be an excellent source of dense calories. I especially like bars that have fruit or nuts added. Just be careful not eat too much at once! I limit my consumption to about 1 ounce (28 g) at a time and not more than once an hour.

- Exercise doesn't have to be high intensity. Find activities you like to do and simply do them more often. If you're curious about a certain activity, such as swimming or martial arts, take a class. If you like what you are doing you are more likely to do it, just like with healthy eating.

- Eating after you work out is very important to replace lost calories. Eating phytochemical-rich foods such as cacao and berries helps to repair damaged cells from a hard workout. Consider any of the recipes in this book as great postworkout meals!

CHAPTER SIX

Recipes at a Glance

Double Pain au Chocolat

Let's get ambitious here for a minute and make chocolate bread. If you are new to baking bread or eating savory chocolate, this is the recipe for you. Here cocoa powder and dark chocolate combine with one of the simplest, most satisfying foods to make—bread. The benefits and taste of cacao shine next to the simplicity of homemade bread.

1 teaspoon dry active yeast

¾ to 1 cup (175 to 235 ml) warm water

1 tablespoon (15 ml) olive oil

1 teaspoon salt

2 teaspoons lemon juice

⅓ cup (27 g) cocoa powder

2 cups (250 g) unbleached white flour

8 ounces (225 g) chocolate, shaved

Activate the yeast by combining it with the warm water and the olive oil in a large mixing bowl and letting it sit for 10 minutes. Stir in the salt, lemon juice, cocoa powder, and flour and work it into a dough. Knead for 5 minutes. Set in a warm place, covered, until doubled in size, which will take about 2 hours.

Punch down the dough and roll it out into two 12-inch (30 cm) baguette shapes on a greased board. Cover gently with oiled plastic wrap and let it rise again for 2 hours. Punch down, twist the dough, and then form it into baguette shapes again with your hands. Score deeply with a knife.

Preheat the oven to 450°F (230°C, gas mark 8).

Place the loaves in lightly greased baguette pans or on a baking sheet and allow to rise while the oven preheats. Sprinkle the loaves with a little water. Bake for about 20 minutes or until browned and crispy. Allow to cool for 10 minutes on a wire rack, then split them open lengthwise, lay in the chocolate shavings, and close. Cut into slices and serve.

Yield: 8 servings

Mashed Cocoa Sweet Potatoes

Sweet potatoes, with their deep-orange, beta-carotene-filled insides, make for wonderful, fiber- and potassium-rich mashed potatoes. Their sweet earthiness is a natural complement to any form of cacao.

¼ cup (40 g) diced onions

2 to 3 tablespoons (28 to 45 ml) olive oil or melted coconut oil, divided

3 cups (675 g) warm, cooked sweet potatoes

2 pressed garlic cloves

½ teaspoon crushed coriander seed

¼ cup (60 g) coconut cream

1 tablespoon (16 g) chipotle paste

¼ cup (20 g) cocoa powder

¼ cup (60 ml) pineapple juice

Salt and black pepper, to taste

1 to 2 tablespoons (1 to 2 g) minced fresh cilantro

Add the onions and 1 tablespoon (15 ml) of oil with a little salt and pepper to a medium skillet over medium-high heat. Sauté until browned, around 3 to 4 minutes, and set aside.

Mash the cooked sweet potatoes in a large mixing bowl with the garlic and then mix in the remaining oil, sautéed onions, coriander, coconut cream, chipotle, cocoa, pineapple juice, salt, and pepper. Adjust seasonings to taste. Sprinkle with the cilantro. Serve immediately.

VARIATIONS: Use unsweetened cocoa powder for a more adult flavor or, if you prefer, slightly sweetened cocoa. Also, add your favorite herbs when you fold in the cilantro.

Yield: 4 servings

Chocolate-Pineapple Egg Rolls

Oh MANganese these egg rolls are good! Pineapples are a great source of manganese, vitamin C, and fiber. Combined with cacao, they make a playful combination of savory and natural sweetness in a crispy treat guaranteed to make your dinner guests happy. The fried option can be an occasional indulgence, or opt for the following Fresh Spring Roll version.

1 tablespoon (8 g) sesame seeds

½ cup (80 g) shredded fresh pineapple, drained

⅓ cup (33 g) shredded unsweetened or bittersweet chocolate

2 tablespoons (20 g) minced red onion

¼ cup (28 g) shredded carrot

2 tablespoons (5 g) minced fresh Thai basil

2 tablespoons (2 g) minced fresh cilantro

2 tablespoons (12 g) minced scallions

1 teaspoon minced or grated fresh ginger

½ teaspoon grated lime peel

1 teaspoon rice vinegar

1 teaspoon tamari or soy sauce

1 cup (248 g) seasoned tofu (precooked, such as 5 Spice, is preferable), cut into strips

¼ teaspoon chile flakes or 1 teaspoon minced or thinly sliced fresh chile pepper (optional)

Salt and black pepper, to taste

16 egg roll wrappers (at least 6 × 6 inches [15 × 15 cm])

Peanut or grapeseed oil, for frying

Toast the sesame seeds in a dry pan over medium heat for 2 to 3 minutes, stirring and turning occasionally, until browned.

In a large bowl, mix together all the ingredients except the salt, pepper, egg roll wrappers, and oil. Season with salt and pepper.

Place 1 wrapper on a cutting board or other flat surface, with one of the points facing you, and add 2 tablespoons (28 g) of the filling about 2 inches (5 cm) from the point nearest you. Tightly roll the wrapper from corner to corner over the dollop (rolling away from you). When you are about a third of the way through rolling up, fold the two side corners inward over the rolled-up dollop so that the points are touching each other and continue rolling. Repeat this process for all of them.

If using a deep fryer, heat 4 or 5 inches (10 or 13 cm) of oil to 350°F (180°C, gas mark 4) and fry the egg rolls in batches for 2 to 3 minutes, turning once with long metal tongs. Drain on absorbent paper.

For stovetop deep frying, add 2 inches (5 cm) of oil to a deep pan, wok, or heavy pot over medium-high heat and cook and turn for the same amount of time or until browned and crispy.

For frying, heat ¼ to ½ inch (6 mm to 1 cm) of oil over medium-high heat in a frying or sauté pan and cook the egg rolls in batches, turning with tongs until all sides are browned, about 4 minutes all together (about 1 minute per side).

Serve these with Chocolate Balsamic Reduction (page 107), chile sauce, a sweet chutney—or all of them!! They are also great sprinkled with additional toasted sesame seeds or rolled in toasted ground peanuts.

Yield: 8 servings

Fresh Spring Roll Option

Add more herbs and fresh mint to this version and use the dry, round rice or tapioca wrappers instead of egg roll wrappers. To prepare these, dip 1 wrapper at a time in cold water or run cold water over it to coat it. Shake the water off. Place on a dry surface and put 2 tablespoons (28 g) of the filling about 1 inch (2.5 cm) from the edge nearest you and wait briefly (less than 30 seconds) for the wrapper to become pliant enough to roll; otherwise, it will break. From there, the rolling process is similar, except you are dealing with a circle rather than a square.

It takes a few tries to get the hang of it and to figure out when the moment to roll is perfect; if you wait too long, the wrapper becomes sticky, too soon and it breaks. Serve when finished. Note: These wrappers are inexpensive and very useful for filling with all sorts of fresh veggies and salads.

Crowd-Pleasing Bell Pepper Pizza

We would be remiss not to include a pizza in here, and the melted chocolate on top is to die for! Pizza may never be a health food, but topping it with dark chocolate, bell peppers, and other vegetables plus fresh basil sure makes a good argument! Plus you get a crust recipe useful for any pizza situation. You're welcome.

FOR THE DOUGH:

2 envelopes rapid rise yeast

⅔ cup (160 ml) warm water (more or less as needed)

2½ cups (313 g) unbleached white flour

⅓ cup (27 g) cocoa powder

1 teaspoon garlic powder

1 teaspoon salt, or to taste

2 tablespoons (28 ml) olive oil

1 teaspoon garlic powder or granulated garlic

¼ cup (35 g) cornmeal

FOR THE SAUCE:

1 cup (245 g) tomato sauce or (240 g) crushed tomatoes

¼ teaspoon salt

⅓ cup (27 g) cocoa powder

⅓ cup (60 g) roasted red bell pepper

1 teaspoon balsamic vinegar

1 tablespoon (15 ml) olive oil

2 crushed garlic cloves

½ teaspoon oregano (dried) or use 1 teaspoon fresh

FOR THE TOPPINGS:

1 cup (150 g) thinly sliced red bell pepper (Roasted are great!)

1 cup (112 g) grated favorite nondairy cheese

1 teaspoon capers

⅓ cup (55 g) diced or sliced red onion

½ cup (57 g) sliced black or kalamata olives

⅓ cup (13 g) sliced basil leaves

¼ to ½ cup (25 to 50 g) thinly sliced or medallions of dark chocolate

TO MAKE THE DOUGH: In a large mixing bowl, stir the yeast into the warm water to dissolve and let sit for 10 to 15 minutes. Mix in the remaining dough ingredients, adding more flour if needed to make a pliable pizza dough. Knead for a few minutes, then place in a bowl in a warm

(Continued on page 158)

place, cover loosely with a cloth, and let rise for 45 minutes or more. You can make a few pizzas with this much dough. Store them in the fridge or freezer to be thawed later for use. Note: If you want to make all of the pizzas at once, double (or triple) the sauce and toppings.

TO MAKE THE SAUCE: Blend all the ingredients together and adjust seasonings to taste. Set aside.

TO MAKE THE PIZZA: Preheat the oven to 425°F (220°C, gas mark 7). Lightly grease a pizza pan or stone and dust with cornmeal. Set aside. Take ⅓ of the dough and roll it out on a surface dusted with flour or cornmeal so that it fits your pizza pan or stone. Place it on the pan or stone and slather evenly with sauce. Add all the toppings except for the chocolate. Bake for about 25 minutes and then add the chocolate pieces and either remove from the oven or allow to cook for another minute. The chocolate will melt into the top and is absolutely delicious. Serve.

Yield: 8 servings

Three Fabulous Cacao Uncheeses (or Pâté) for Cheez Plate

These recipes are strong, unusual, and definitely worth playing around with. I'm the sort who eats curry paste or miso on toast. These are meant to be very intense (and pretty salty) flavors and should be served with crackers, little toasts, agave nectar, sliced fruit (pears and apples in particular), crudités, toasted almonds, sliced beets, and other things normally associated with a cheese plate. Using miso, sauerkraut, and cider vinegar gives these a natural fermented flavor.

Miso-Cacao

¼ cup (64 g) miso paste

⅓ cup (32 g) raw cacao powder

1 tablespoon (15 ml) rice vinegar, or more to taste

1 tablespoon (15 ml) almond or other oil

¼ cup (25 g) chopped scallions

Blend all the ingredients in a food processor until fairly smooth. Season to taste and chill.

Yield: 4 servings

Sauerkraut-Dark Chocolate

4 ounces (115 g) dark chocolate

½ cup (71 g) sauerkraut

2 crushed peeled garlic cloves

¼ cup (24 g) nutritional yeast

½ teaspoon salt, or to taste

1 tablespoon (15 ml) olive oil

1 tablespoon (15 ml) lemon juice

Melt the chocolate over low heat in a double boiler. Remove, add with the remaining ingredients to a food processor, and blend until smooth. Chill.

Yield: 4 servings

Curry-Bittersweet Cocoa-Tahini

4 ounces (115 g) bittersweet chocolate

2 tablespoons (30 g) mild curry paste

2 tablespoons (10 g) cocoa powder

1 tablespoon (15 ml) cider vinegar, or to taste

1 tablespoon (15 ml) tamari, or to taste

1 tablespoon (7 g) powdered coconut

2 tablespoons (16 g) toasted sesame seeds or 1 tablespoon (15 g) tahini

Melt the chocolate over low heat in a double boiler. Remove, add to a food processor with the remaining ingredients, and blend. Chill.

Yield: 4 servings

Flavanol-Full Chocolate Pudding

Hazelnuts are quite tasty, and their cohabitation with chocolate is only natural. We see hazelnuts paired with chocolate for truffles and in the well-known spread Nutella. They also pair together as a great source of the phytochemical group flavanols.

⅓ cup (107 g) hazelnut syrup

1 teaspoon vanilla extract

Pinch or two salt

¼ cup (20 g) cocoa powder

2 cups (475 ml) chocolate soy milk or other chocolate milk, divided

1 cup (132 g) melted chocolate

¼ cup (30 g) tapioca starch

Candied hazelnuts and shaved chocolate for garnishing

In a large saucepan over low to medium heat, whisk the syrup, vanilla, salt, cocoa powder, and 1½ cups (355 ml) of the milk into the melted chocolate. Cook, stirring a bit, until it begins to simmer. Reduce the heat. In a small bowl, blend the tapioca starch with the rest of the milk. Stir this into the pudding and cook for 10 minutes or until it begins to thicken. Pour into a large bowl and chill in the refrigerator, stirring occasionally, until cold, about 4 to 6 hours. Serve with grated chocolate and candied hazelnuts on top. The Cocoa-Coconut Cream (page 173) is also a great topping, of course!

Yield: 4 servings

Basic Double Chocolate Sauce

Ah, necessities! Make your own chocolate sauce with high-quality chocolate and know that you are getting the most out of the cacao bean. And like cacao, coconut is a good source of magnesium. Many people don't meet the recommended daily intake for this essential mineral, another great reason to eat cacao and coconut. With this recipe, you have the ability to adjust the sweetness as desired. This can be used with all sorts of delights from ice cream, pie, trifle, and fruit to pieces of cake.

1 cup (170 g) chopped bittersweet chocolate or (175 g) chocolate chips

½ cup (120 ml) chocolate, coconut, or soy milk (or other)

2 tablespoons (40 g) syrup, such as agave, sugar, or maple (optional)

2 tablespoons (10 g) cocoa powder

Pinch of salt

In a heavy medium-size saucepan, melt the chocolate in the chocolate milk over low heat, stirring, and then whisk in the rest of the ingredients. When the mixture cools, add more liquid as needed to keep a saucy texture and adjust the sweetener as desired. As an alternative, this recipe can be made in a double boiler.

Yield: 6 servings

Cocoa Buffalo Tempura Vegetables

The cocoa adds a slightly candied quality to the batter for these. Armed with the basic idea of chili and chocolate for dipping, broccoli and sweet potatoes, some of the healthiest, most nutrient-dense vegetables you can eat, lend themselves nicely to being battered. Common in some Indian and Japanese cooking, battered vegetables are a fun, creative way to eat them.

FOR THE BATTER:

1 cup (125 g) unbleached white flour
(or mix half rice flour, half regular)

1 teaspoon salt

1 teaspoon sugar

1 teaspoon baking powder or soda

1/3 cup (27 g) cocoa powder

1 teaspoon curry powder

1 teaspoon garlic powder

1¼ cups (285 ml) beer or soda water,
or to taste

FOR THE VEGGIES:

1 cup (110 g) thinly sliced sweet potato

1 cup (71 g) broccoli crown pieces

1 cup (160 g) onion rings

8 whole cremini mushrooms

Oil, for frying

FOR THE SERVING SAUCE:

1/3 cup (80 ml) your favorite hot sauce

1/4 cup (20 g) cocoa powder

1/2 teaspoon salt

1 tablespoon (15 ml) olive oil

1/4 cup (60 ml) cider or malt vinegar

2 crushed garlic cloves

1 teaspoon onion powder

1/2 teaspoon each chili powder
and paprika

TO MAKE THE BATTER: Mix together all
the batter ingredients in a large bowl until you end up with a consistency similar
to pancake batter.

TO MAKE THE VEGGIES: Dip the veggies
in the batter, coating well. Depending
on the size of the vegetables used, it
may be necessary to make more batter.
Heat about 1 inch (2.5 cm) of oil over
medium-high heat in a deep skillet. Add
the coated vegetables, being sure not
to crowd the pan. Fry, turning once and
cooking until crispy on both sides, for
about 2 minutes per side. Alternatively,
cook them in a deep fryer or bake them
using a light brushing of oil on a greased
baking pan at 425°F (220°C, gas mark 7),
turning once, for 20 minutes. Drain on
absorbent paper.

TO MAKE THE SERVING SAUCE: Blend all
the ingredients together in a blender
or food processor. Adjust seasonings
to taste. Experiment with this one!

Yield: 8 servings

Dairy-Free Double Chocolate Cookies

It is unusual to see a recipe for one dozen cookies, but I thought I'd be a friend to those who don't want to eat zillions of cookies every time they make them. These will make you feel naughty! Because they are as decadent and delicious as you imagine them. This is not your everyday chocolate cookie, and you'll be amazed that they are egg and dairy free, which means they are also cholesterol free!

1 cup (125 g) unbleached white flour

2 teaspoons baking powder

½ cup (40 g) cocoa powder

½ teaspoon salt

½ cup (112 g) vegan margarine
(or oil of choice, such as coconut)

⅔ cup (133 g) sugar

¼ cup (60 ml) soy milk, almond milk, or other (Vanilla or chocolate flavor is great!)

¾ cup (131 g) semisweet or bittersweet chocolate chips

Preheat the oven to 350°F (180°C, gas mark 4).

Mix the flour, powders, and salt together in a large mixing bowl. In another mixing bowl, cream the margarine, sugar, and milk together. Gently mix the wet into the dry and then fold in the chocolate chips. Try not to eat it all now!

Separate the dough into 12 balls and place them on a lightly greased baking sheet. Press down gently on each to flatten slightly. Bake for approximately 14 minutes. Keep an eye that they don't burn or become overcooked. They will have a modestly soft crunch on the outside, be chewy and moist on the inside, and are as chocolaty as can be. It's hard not to just eat them all at once.

Remove from the oven and place the baking sheet on a wire rack. After 2 minutes, use a spatula to make sure you can get all of them off, but don't actually remove them yet. (You're just moving them around to make sure they don't stick to the rack while cooling.) Cool until warm and devour; they are also good at room temperature but to die for when warm.

VARIATION: Roll the balls of dough in cinnamon and cocoa or cinnamon sugar before baking for a slight kick.

Yield: 6 servings

Dolmades with Chocolate-Currant Rice and Cocoa-Coconut Tzatziki

For the uninitiated, dolmades, or dolmas, are grape leaves typically stuffed with seasoned rice or meat. Grape leaves are pretty exciting and contain a good dose of vitamin A for starters. And tzatziki made from coconut and raw cacao powder is so creamy and delicious that you'll want to put it on everything!

FOR THE DOLMADES:

1 cup (165 g) cooked rice mixed with seasoning of your choice

¼ cup (38 g) dried currants

2 tablespoons (20 g) minced red onion

1 teaspoon minced fresh ginger

¼ teaspoon salt, or to taste

¼ teaspoon red chile flakes

¼ cup (4 g) minced fresh cilantro or (16 g) Italian parsley

2 teaspoons cider vinegar

1 teaspoon olive oil

¼ cup (33 g) grated bittersweet chocolate

2 tablespoons (14 g) grated carrot

12 grape leaves

FOR THE TZATZIKI:

½ cup (120 g) coconut cream

2 tablespoons (28 ml) lemon juice

2 tablespoons (12 g) raw cacao powder

1 tablespoon (15 ml) olive oil

½ teaspoon salt

1 crushed garlic clove

1 teaspoon chopped fresh dill

¼ cup (35 g) peeled, chopped cucumber

TO MAKE THE DOLMADES: In a medium bowl, mix the rice through the grated carrot. Place a grape leaf on a flat surface with the base facing you. Place 2 tablespoons (28 g) of filling close to the edge of the base. Roll tightly away from you, folding the edges in to cover the ends of the filling after the first fold. Chill.

TO MAKE THE TZATZIKI: Blend the coconut cream, lemon juice, cacao, olive oil, salt, and garlic until smooth in a food processor or blender. Add the dill and cucumber and season to taste. Serve with the dolmades. You can drizzle or spoon this on top or serve on the side for dipping.

VARIATION: Blanched, drained chard or collard leaves work well as an alternative to the grape leaves.

Yield: 6 servings

Nondairy Chocolate Wontons

Should they be savory? Should they be sweet? The choice is yours! Eat your heart out, crab rangoon! The type of nondairy cream cheese you use will determine the flavor and nutritional composition of these wontons. Tofu, bean (such as cannellini or butter beans) with lemon juice, coconut, nut, or even potato or taro root can be used to make nondairy "cream cheese." One of the beautiful things about vegetable-based cuisine is that nearly anything can be made into nearly anything!

½ cup (65 g) grated bittersweet chocolate

½ cup (115 g) your favorite nondairy cream cheese

¼ cup (65 g) mango chutney

16 wonton wrappers (4 × 4 inch, or 10 × 10 cm each)

Oil, for frying

Mix the chocolate, cream cheese, and chutney together. Place a tablespoon-size (15 g) dollop on a wonton wrapper close to the corner and roll tightly using the same method as with an egg roll (see Chocolate-Pineapple Egg Rolls on page 156). Repeat with all the wrappers.

Heat 4 to 5 inches (10 to 13 cm) of oil in a deep fryer (or 2 inches [5 cm] in a deep pan, wok, or sturdy pot on medium-high on the stovetop). Place each wonton into the fryer, turning once, until browned, approximately 2 to 3 minutes. Drain on absorbent paper.

VARIATIONS: Send these flavors in either a sweet or savory direction depending on which chocolate, chutney, and cream cheese you use. For sweetness, dust with cinnamon-cocoa sugar. For savory wontons, dust with a seasoned salt or curry–cocoa powder mixture.

SUGGESTIONS: For an interesting presentation, serve with sliced Asian pear sprinkled with a little ginger. Also, use any uncooked leftover filling by placing a dot on top of each wonton before serving. Or serve with chile sauce.

Yield: 8 servings

Apricot Brownies with Beta-Carotene

Apricots are great by themselves and are especially good with chocolate. This is a fun recipe that combines the fat-soluble beta-carotene found in apricots nicely with the healthy fat of cacao and nuts. If adding melted chocolate to the batter makes you nervous, you can substitute ½ cup (88 g) chocolate chips.

⅓ cup (80 ml) canola or melted coconut oil

½ cup (128 g) apricot purée

½ cup (66 g) melted chocolate

½ cup (100 g) sugar, or to taste

1 teaspoon vanilla extract

½ cup chopped nuts ([30 g] walnuts, [28 g] pecans, [35 g] cashews, or [31 g] pistachios)

¼ cup (33 g) chopped dried apricots

1½ cups (188 g) unbleached white flour

½ teaspoon salt, or to taste

1½ teaspoons baking powder

⅓ cup (27 g) cocoa powder

Preheat the oven to 350°F (180°C, gas mark 4). Grease and lightly flour an 8- × 8-inch (20 × 20 cm) cake pan and set aside.

Blend the oil, apricot purée, melted chocolate, sugar, and vanilla together in a large mixing bowl. Fold in the nuts and dried apricots.

In another mixing bowl, mix or sift together the flour, salt, baking powder, and cocoa powder. Slowly stir the dry mixture into the liquid mixture. Transfer to the cake pan and bake for about 30 minutes. Remove, cool, and cut into 16 squares.

Yield: 8 servings

Chocolate Capsaicin Cake

This not-too-sweet cake evokes the original seasonings of Meso-america and adds a zing with jalapeños. Capsaicin, the active compound in jalapeños that makes them spicy, also helps you to burn more calories, one study found. Does that mean you should eat this chocolate cake to lose weight? No. But now you have an interesting fact to explain why there are jalapeños in your cake. If you choose not to use jalapeño, it just becomes a regular basic vegan chocolate cake recipe, sans interesting fact.

1 cup (200 g) sugar or your favorite sweetener, or to taste

1¾ cups (219 g) unbleached white flour

¾ cup (60 g) cocoa powder

1½ teaspoons baking powder

1½ teaspoons baking soda

1 teaspoon salt

1½ teaspoons ground cinnamon

½ teaspoon ground ginger

1 cup (235 ml) coconut, soy, nut, or oat milk

⅓ cup (80 ml) canola or grapeseed oil

1 tablespoon (15 ml) lime juice

1½ teaspoons vanilla

1 tablespoon (6 g) minced jalapeño, or to taste

1 cup (235 ml) hot water

½ cup (88 g) bittersweet chocolate chips (optional)

Preheat the oven to 350°F (180°C, gas mark 4). Grease and flour two 9-inch (23 cm) round baking pans.

Stir together the sugar, flour, cocoa and baking powders, baking soda, salt, cinnamon, and ginger in a large mixing bowl.

Add the coconut milk, oil, lime juice, vanilla, and jalapeño; beat for a few minutes until incorporated. Stir in the hot water. Stir in chocolate chips now if you are using them. Pour the batter into the prepared pans. Bake 35 to 40 minutes or until done (use the toothpick test). Cool 10 to 15 minutes and then remove from the pans and cool on wire racks. Cool completely before frosting (if using).

NOTE: As an alternative to frosting, drizzle the cake with a spicy agave syrup or sprinkle with powdered seasoned cocoa.

Yield: 8 servings

Simple Yet Effective Trifle

Trifle is a quite pleasing dessert and a great finish to a meal if you're trying to impress friends with an adult treat. And whenever the sweetness of those phytochemical-rich berries meets the fatty goodness of cacao, you know it's going to be a good time.

½ cup (88 g) semisweet or bittersweet chocolate chips

¾ cup (175 ml) your favorite nondairy cream or milk

2 cups (70 g) chocolate cake or cookies of your choice, chopped into large pieces

⅓ cup (107 g) jam (I like apricot, blackberry, or raspberry.)

¼ teaspoon each ground cloves and ginger

¼ cup (20 g) cocoa powder, ½ teaspoon ground cinnamon, and 1 tablespoon (13 g) sugar mixed together, divided

1½ cups (190 g) raspberries (or other favorite berry)

1 cup Cocoa-Coconut Cream (page 173)

¼ cup (25 g) shaved chocolate

Melt the chocolate chips into the cream or milk over low heat in a heavy saucepan or double boiler. While the chocolate melts, place the cake or cookies in an 8-inch (20 cm) casserole or soufflé dish (or use ramekins or glasses for individual servings). Pour the chocolate sauce over the pieces. Place in the refrigerator and allow to chill for 20 minutes.

Next, mix the jam with the cloves and ginger in a bowl and spread on top of the cake layer. Sprinkle with some of the cocoa, cinnamon, and sugar mixture. Pour the berries on top and sprinkle with more of the cocoa, cinnamon, and sugar. Layer the Coconut Cocoa Cream on top and again sprinkle with the cinnamon, cocoa, and sugar. Sprinkle the shaved chocolate on top. Chill until you're ready to serve.

VARIATION: I sprinkle alcohol on my trifle liberally. If you would like to do so, use 3 or 4 tablespoons (45 or 60 ml) of dessert wine, crème de cassis, or other suitable liqueur and sprinkle this onto the cake or cookie pieces in the dish before adding everything else.

Yield: 6 servings

Do-It-Yourself Cocoa Piecrust

This is a go-to piecrust for all things pie. For sweets, keep it so. For savory, simply omit the sugar!

2 tablespoons (26 g) sugar

¼ cup (20 g) sweetened or unsweetened cocoa powder

1¼ cups (156 g) sifted unbleached white flour

¼ teaspoon salt

½ cup (112 g) cold vegan margarine

3 to 4 tablespoons (45 to 60 ml) cold water

Preheat the oven 425°F (220°C, gas mark 7).

Mix the sugar, cocoa powder, flour, and salt together in a large mixing bowl.

Cut in the margarine until the mixture resembles coarse crumbs. Add water by mixing it in by the tablespoon (15 ml) until you can form a malleable ball. Roll out the dough to fit into lightly greased pie pans and press in gently. Prick here and there with a fork. Bake for 20 to 25 minutes or until browned. This recipe makes two crusts.

VARIATION: Use oil instead of margarine when making the dough. You'll need slightly less than ½ cup (120 ml). Melted coconut oil would be great, for example.

Yield: 2 piecrusts

Cashew Calcium Shake

This delicious shake is hard to dislike. Sesame seeds are especially good for you if you can find the unhulled kind because they contain significantly more calcium than regular, hulled sesame seeds. Just 1 ounce (28 g) of unhulled sesame seeds gives you 25 percent of the Daily Value for both calcium and iron!

⅓ cup (27 g) cocoa powder

¼ cup (33 g) melted chocolate

1 cup (140 g) cashews

2 tablespoons (16 g) sesame seeds, preferably unhulled

Pinch of salt

½ teaspoon vanilla extract

¼ cup (50 g) sugar or (80 g) syrup

(such as agave), or to taste

2 cups (475 ml) chocolate coconut or soy milk

Blend all the ingredients in a blender until smooth. Chill and blend again before serving. This shake can also be partially frozen and then blended.

Yield: 2 servings

Plum Power Pudding Pie

Plums are a very good source of vitamin C. The iron found in chocolate needs vitamin C for improved absorption.

1 unbaked Cocoa Piecrust (page 172), using half almond flour and half regular flour

1 cup (132 g) melted chocolate

1 cup (256 g) puréed plums

½ cup (100 g) sugar

¼ cup (60 ml) apple juice

½ cup (56 g) almond flour

⅓ cup (50 g) golden raisins, chopped

1 tablespoon (6 g) grated orange peel

1 teaspoon vanilla

½ teaspoon salt

1 tablespoon (8 g) tapioca starch

Reserved sliced plums, melted chocolate, and orange peel ribbons, for garnish

1 recipe Cocoa-Coconut Cream (below)

Preheat the oven to 425°F (220°C, gas mark 7).

Roll out the crust and press gently into a lightly greased 10-inch (25 cm) pie pan (cut off any excess crust). Mix together the chocolate through the tapioca starch in a large mixing bowl and pour into the piecrust. Bake for 10 minutes, lower the heat to 350°F (180°C, gas mark 4), and bake for 20 minutes more. Cool and garnish. Serve with Cocoa-Coconut Cream.

Yield: 8 servings

Cocoa-Coconut Cream

This cream is great for desserts, by itself, or frozen. You can adjust sweetness and other seasonings and mix or replace the coconut with applesauce, avocados, nut butters, and other creamy or saucy things to your great delight!

⅓ cup (27 g) raw or regular cocoa powder

1 cup (240 g) coconut cream

¼ cup (33 g) melted bittersweet chocolate

Pinch salt

½ teaspoon vanilla

1 tablespoon (14 g) coconut oil

1 tablespoon (15 ml) lemon juice

¼ cup (50 g) sugar or (80 g) syrup (such as agave)

Blend all the ingredients together until smooth. Chill.

NOTE: When using coconut cream, make sure you're using the thick cream on top, not the milk.

Yield: 6 servings

Blueberry-Cocoa Beneficial Bites

Blueberries, bananas, and chocolate—what could possibly be better? I've added healthful, helpful papaya, that's what! The deep orange color of papaya tells you that it is full of beneficial carotenoids, but that's not the only phytochemical present. Like tomatoes, papaya is a good source of cancer-fighting lycopene. With blueberries' anthocyanins, cacao's flavanols, and papaya's carotenoids and lycopene, these bites are a powerful cocktail of disease-fighting goodness!

½ cup (75 g) dried bananas

½ cup (73 g) mixed nuts

¼ cup (33 g) dried papaya

¼ cup (24 g) cacao powder

½ cup (60 g) dried blueberries

2 tablespoons (26 g) cacao butter, plus more as needed

1 or 2 tablespoons (20 or 40 g) agave nectar or other sweetener

¼ teaspoon salt, or to taste

Grind the bananas, nuts, and papaya together in a food processor. Add the rest of the ingredients and process. Remove from the blender and form into 16 small balls. Roll in cacao powder or coconut flakes. Chill and serve.

Yield: 4 servings

Chronic-Disease-Walloping Bars

This one's a beast that can start your day out right. Sure, oats contain lots of that cholesterol-lowering fiber, but who wants to eat plain ol' oatmeal when you can make these Choco Wallop Bars and keep them in the fridge ready to go? Nuts aid in the fight against heart disease along with cacao and oats and come together to make this a tasty, healthy treat you can eat anytime.

2 cups (160 g) oats

1 cup (110 g) mixed sliced almonds and chopped Brazil nuts

1 cup (85 g) shredded dried coconut

½ cup (40 g) cocoa powder

3 tablespoons (42 g) coconut oil

½ cup (168 g) agave nectar, maple syrup, or (100 g) coconut sugar

½ cup (130 g) peanut butter, cashew, or almond butter

1 teaspoon vanilla extract or scrapings of 1 bean

¼ teaspoon salt, or to taste

½ cup (89 g) chopped pitted dates

½ cup (65 g) chopped dried mango

½ cup (75 g) golden raisins or currants

½ cup (85 g) chopped dark chocolate + 1 tablespoon (14 g) coconut oil

Preheat the oven to 350°F (180°C, gas mark 4). Grease a 9- × 13-inch (23 × 33 cm) baking dish and line with parchment paper.

Toss the oats, nuts, and coconut together on a baking sheet and bake for 10 to 12 minutes, stirring occasionally, until lightly browned. Transfer the mixture to a large mixing bowl and stir in the cocoa powder.

Reduce the oven temperature to 300°F (150°C, gas mark 2).

Place the oil, sweetener, nut butter, vanilla, and salt in a saucepan and bring to a boil over medium heat. Cook and stir for a minute and then pour over the toasted oatmeal mixture. Add the dates, mango, and raisins and stir well. Pour the mixture into the greased pan and press evenly into the pan. Bake for 25 minutes until browned. Cool for a few hours and cut into 16 bars.

Melt the chocolate in a double boiler with the coconut oil. Place in a shallow bowl and lightly dip the bottoms of the bars in this mixture. Cool bottom-side up.

Yield: 8 servings

Coconut Shortbread–Double Brownie Delight

This has been my potluck special of late. An amazing coconut shortbread combines with an extra-chocolaty, moist brownie to make a decadent, delicious double-decked delight. Desserts need not be totally avoided in a healthy diet; discretionary calories exist, and a cacao-coconut treat is a great way to use them. This treat is so rich and delicious, you only need a small piece to satisfy your sweet tooth.

FOR THE SHORTBREAD LAYER:

1⅔ cups (208 g) unbleached white flour

⅓ cup (27 g) cocoa powder

⅔ cup (133 g) sugar

½ teaspoon salt, or to taste

½ cup (112 g) coconut oil

2 teaspoons vanilla

2 tablespoons (28 ml) coconut milk or water, or as needed

FOR THE BROWNIE LAYER:

½ cup (40 g) cocoa powder

½ cup (63 g) unbleached white flour

¼ teaspoon salt

1½ teaspoons baking powder

¼ cup (56 g) coconut oil

⅔ cup (133 g) sugar

½ cup (120 ml) soy or coconut milk

1 teaspoon vanilla extract

4 ounces (115 g) chopped bittersweet or dark chocolate pieces

Preheat the oven to 375°F (190°C, gas mark 5).

TO MAKE THE SHORTBREAD LAYER: Mix the dry shortbread ingredients in a large mixing bowl and then add the coconut oil and incorporate with your hands to make crumbs. Add the rest of the liquid and press into a lightly greased 8- × 8-inch (20 × 20 cm) pan. Score with a fork.

TO MAKE THE BROWNIE LAYER: Mix the dry brownie ingredients together in a large mixing bowl, add the wet ingredients and the chocolate chips, and combine to make a nice batter. Pour over the top of the shortbread. Bake for about 35 minutes or until done to your liking. Cool on a wire rack and then cut into 16 squares.

Yield: 8 servings

Raw Cacao Phyto-Power Blocks

Goji berries are a delightful superfood loaded with vitamins and carotenoids such as beta-carotene and lycopene. Combined with the flavanols from the cacao, you have some preposterously phytochemical-packed power blocks here. These mildly sweet chews bring to mind Fig Newtons, Turkish delight, and other yummy treats, yet they are considerably more healthful thanks to the nuts, goji berries, and of course, cacao.

¾ cup (75 g) pecans, walnuts, or other nuts

⅓ cup (75 g) raw cacao nibs

1 tablespoon (8 g) sesame seeds

½ cup (89 g) pitted dates

½ cup (65 g) dried apricots or pineapple

¼ cup (23 g) dried goji berries

1 tablespoon (20 g) maple syrup or agave nectar

Pinch salt

Line an 8- × 8-inch (20 × 20 cm) baking dish with wax paper. Set aside.

In a food processor, grind the nuts, cacao, and sesame seeds. The substance should be fairly fine, like bread crumbs. Remove and set aside. Next, process the dates and fruit until you reach a chunky texture. Add the nut mixture back in and process for another minute or until clumpy. In a medium bowl, mix with a spoon, adding maple syrup and salt to taste. Press into your prepared baking dish. Chill for 30 minutes, cut into 16 squares, and serve or store. Use more nuts or less fruit for drier cubes.

Yield: 8 servings

Cacao Sugar Scrub

This recipe is more for your feet or face than your mouth! Keep your nice, sexy complexion youthful, my dears. The gritty sugar and cacao help to exfoliate, while the herbs and cacao soothe and smooth. Double-acting cacao, it's such a treasure!

¼ cup (24 g) raw cacao powder

½ cup (112 g) coconut oil or almond oil (You could also use cocoa butter, of course.)

¾ cup (150 g) sugar

¼ cup (6 g) dried crushed mint, lemon verbena, or other soothing herbal leaves

Mix all the ingredients together with a mortar and pestle or food processor. Use as a foot scrub. Both the sugar and the cacao will act to exfoliate.

VARIATIONS: Can you make a salt scrub with cacao? Sure you can! Replace the sugar with salt. Also, add a few drops of essential oils such as lavender.

Yield: 4 applications

Fair What? Raw How? Picking the Right Cacao for You

Choosing and buying the best chocolate for you, the environment, and the people who grow it can seem daunting. There is an array of cacao and chocolate on the market, not to mention the numerous accompanying label certifications and standards. Some certifications, such as organic, are federally protected and managed, while others have no standards behind them and tend to obfuscate the real issues. And some smaller companies will say anything to get you to believe that their product is healthier/better/more ethical than that of their competitors.

The best we can do is to educate ourselves on the issues and decide which factors are most important to each of us. And like anything, the ideal scenario may not always be plausible, but as cacao and fine chocolate become more popular, our dollars can dictate the direction in which the industry goes.

For Better Quality and Nutrition, Know What You Are Getting

Our food system is unfathomably large and extremely complex. Millions of tons of cacao, worth hundreds of billions of dollars, are grown, processed, shipped, and packaged globally. The scale and complexity of the system make knowing about where your food comes from—and identifying better options—difficult.

Many people try to make informed choices about their food by doing things like shopping at farmer's markets, buying shade-grown coffee, or even just taking the time to read ingredient labels closely. As we make these changes, it's normal to ask, "Does this even make a difference?" My resounding answer is, yes, it does. In the past two decades, the consumer-driven changes to make the food system more transparent, and more ethical, have led to an unprecedented level of awareness.

Now, before you get too excited, remember this is just the beginning. We *know* more about our food and where it comes from, but there are still many barriers to overcome to make the necessary changes to become fully informed. Fortunately, there are tools for us to use, and my goal with this chapter is to apply them to cacao because higher quality and higher standards lead to better cacao and better nutrition.

Understanding the Labels on Cacao and Chocolate

Chocolate may lead the pack when it comes to certifications, labels, and packaging riddled with claims. (I'm snacking on a dark chocolate bar right now that has no fewer than six certification logos!) These claims show us where and how each chocolate bar came to be. I'll help you make educated decisions and reduce any trepidation you may have about buying nutritious, environmentally friendly, and ethically produced chocolate and cacao. Let's look at the following labels and what they mean.

Health claims. Explicit health claims on packaging are regulated by the Food and Drug Administration (FDA), and there are currently no approved claims for cacao or chocolate. The FDA only regulates the percentage of cocoa solids for the categorizing of chocolate types that we learned about in chapter 1. This fact doesn't keep companies from telling you why their chocolate may be better in other, creative ways.

Natural. In a nutshell, the term *natural* is meaningless. There is no agreed-upon definition and no regulatory control or agency for this term. It is often used in what some people call "health washing": making a food item appear to be healthier than it really is by adding virtually meaningless terms. Don't be fooled by this terminology! Some foods are not what they seem.

Recently, food activists and public health lawyers have taken companies to court over their use of the word *natural* for products containing high fructose corn syrup, genetically engineered ingredients, artificial ingredients or preservatives, or other unnatural ingredients. Because of these actions, the term is being used less often but is still one to keep an eye on.

Raw cacao. There are currently no official labels or third-party regulations for a food to be marked as "raw," but the generally agreed-upon standards for raw food are simply that a food cannot be heated above 118°F/48°C. Raw food advocates claim there are health benefits to eating fruits, vegetables, nuts, seeds, sprouts, and other foods in their natural, uncooked state. Raw cacao beans are not easy to come by but are becoming increasingly available, in part because of the many raw food advocates who are pushing for better and increased use of cacao in the diet. Beyond raw cacao, there are even raw chocolates now that use raw cacao powder, cacao butter, and minimally processed raw sweeteners to create nutritionally packed, high-antioxidant chocolate bars.

Dutch processed cocoa. On the other end of the spectrum, we have Dutch processed chocolate, which is treated with an alkalizing agent to reduce the naturally bitter taste of cacao. Invented by Dutch chocolate maker Coenraad Johannes van Houten in the nineteenth century, this process produced a much milder taste that significantly increased the use of cocoa in Europe. Van Houten's father, also a chocolate maker, is responsible for the machinery that first separated cacao butter from cacao beans, essentially making the first cocoa powder. These two processes led to the development of the modern-day chocolate bar.

There is clear evidence that Dutch-processed cocoa powder has fewer active flavonoids than other cacao products: The bitterness in cacao is from the actual flavonoids. What is less clear, however, is how much this matters. The antioxidant capacity of cacao (due to the flavonoids) is so high that even when consuming Dutch-processed cocoa powder, you still consume significant amounts.

On the other hand, because a large portion of cacao consumed is in the form of Dutch-processed cocoa powder, large chocolate companies are interested in associating their product with the health benefits of cacao. My advice is to eat actual cacao—in the form of nibs, cacao powder, and very dark chocolate or non-Dutch-processed cocoa for the most health benefits. Dutch-processed cocoa or other types of chocolate with added ingredients still contain beneficial flavonoids, just to a lesser extent.

Cacao Production and the Environment

The environmental cost of growing, shipping, manufacturing, and getting cacao to consumers will never be zero. But each of these processes can happen in a variety of ways, and options exist to reduce the impact of cacao product consumption on the environment. Let's have a look at some of the most popular labels and certifications.

USDA organic. *Organic* is a labeling term that indicates that the food has been produced through methods approved by the U.S. Department of Agriculture (USDA). These methods integrate cultural, biological, and mechanical practices that foster resourcefulness, promote ecological balance, and conserve biodiversity. Synthetic fertilizers, sewage sludge, irradiation, and genetic engineering may not be used in organic farming.

The USDA certifies and regulates all organic crops and agricultural products through the National Organic Program. Organic certification agencies inspect and verify that organic farmers, distributors, processors, and traders are complying with the established standards. More than ninety organic certification agencies operating around the world certify organic products. To label or represent their products as organic, growers and producers must follow all of the specifications.

Reducing pesticide use is a personal health issue, but also an environmental and social issue. The more organic crops are grown, the fewer total pesticides and chemicals are used worldwide. Organic is a fast-growing industry, and organic cacao is very popular. It's important to note that organic foods do not contain genetically modified organisms (GMOs).

Non-GMO certified. The long-term health and environmental effects of GMOs are unknown; this is reason enough for many people to avoid GMOs for health and philosophical reasons. More than sixty countries ban or require labeling of GMO foods! Currently, no commercially available cacao beans have been genetically engineered, but ingredients found in chocolate may contain GMOs and therefore, you will find certified non-GMO cacao and chocolate.

The Non-GMO Project is a nonprofit organization that certifies non-GMO products and educates consumers about GMOs. The Non-GMO Project's Product Verification Program is a process-based program designed to assess compliance with the Non-GMO Project Standard. The core requirements are traceability, segregation, and testing at critical control points. For more information see its website, www.labelgmos.org.

Rainforest Alliance Certified. Because all cacao is grown close to the equator, plantations are on or near tropical land. The Rainforest Alliance certifies farms that work to reduce the environmental impact on the tropical rain forest. Like coffee, cacao *can* be cultivated using the shade of native trees to maintain a landscape not too dissimilar from the original forested land. Using these trees helps to conserve the native habitat of plants, animals, and birds and keeps biological systems less disturbed. Unfortunately, this approach is rarely taken, as it requires more work and returns less profit from the land. The Rainforest Alliance works with cocoa and chocolate companies to encourage environmentally minded agriculture and certifies farms as such. They look for farms that focus on sustainability and provide decent working conditions.

Cacao Labor and Production Practices:
Looking for Fair, Equal, and Just

In an industry worth tens of billions of dollars, it's not surprising that there is a push to grow and process cacao as fast and profitably as possible. And in the current global economy that unfortunately means paying the people doing the physical labor very low wages. Or sometimes paying them none at all.

In cacao production, exploitative labor is all too common. Because cacao grows in limited regions near the equator, nearly three-quarters of the world's cacao comes from West Africa, mainly Ghana and the Ivory Coast. There are more than 600,000 cacao plantations in the Ivory Coast alone. The labor standards there are poor to nonexistent, and the world's desire for cheap chocolate has exacerbated the situation. Fortunately, there are numerous organizations working diligently to improve the livelihood of those who grow the cacao we know and love.

Fair trade. Fairtrade International (also known as FLO, the acronym of the organization's former name, Fairtrade Labeling Organization International) is one of the first worldwide organizations to work directly with family farmers and workers around the world with the aim of increasing wages and reducing poverty. It is the grandfather organization of equitably purchased foods and ingredients. According to its mission statement, it uses "a market-based approach that empowers farmers to get a fair price for their harvest, helps workers create safe working conditions, provides a decent living wage, and guarantees the right to organize. Through direct, equitable trade, farming and working families are able to eat better, keep their kids in school, improve health and housing, and invest in the future. Keeping families, local economies, the natural environment, and the larger community strong today and for generations to come."

Fair trade is an alternative approach to conventional trade and strives to connect consumers with the producers of their food, even if they are halfway around the world. Fair trade attempts to get producers a better deal on improved terms when their product is bought and sold in the global market. Fair trade offers consumers a way to reduce poverty, not through charity, but via a more equitable market that improves the livelihood of the growers and workers.

There are two distinct sets of fair trade standards. One set of standards applies to smallholders that are working together in cooperatives or other organizations with a democratic structure. The other set applies to workers whose employers pay decent wages, guarantee the right to join trade unions, ensure health and safety standards, and provide adequate housing where relevant. Fair trade standards also cover terms of trade. Most products have a fair trade price, which is the minimum that must be paid to the producers. In addition, producers get an additional sum, the fair trade premium, to invest in their communities.

Fair Trade USA. In 2011, Fair Trade USA left FLO to expand its own program and certification. This included larger farms that had been previously excluded from FLO certification because of their size. Fair Trade USA felt they could improve upon the work that FLO started, and their symbol quickly became recognizable throughout the United States. Critics argue that this move was financially motivated and that Fair Trade USA's interest is in collecting fees from members. Other criticisms of fair trade labeling, by both Fair Trade USA and FLO, is that adherence to standards is poor and enforcement is lacking. Nonetheless, they have laid the groundwork to connect people with the producers of their food and improve the transparency of the food system.

Equal Exchange. Organizations working on labor issues and labeling are not limited to FLO and Fair Trade USA. In 1986, an organization called Equal Exchange was founded to challenge the existing trade model that favors large plantations and large corporations. Like FLO, it supports small farmers and connects consumers and producers through information, education, and the exchange of products in the marketplace. It works closely with alternative traders, small farmers, and nonprofits that have a justice, not charity, focus. Equal Exchange believes that the Fair Trade label has chipped away at the original standards and is no longer as meaningful a certification as it once was. The Equal Exchange label is an alternative to Fair Trade USA if you share the same concerns and want to support smaller farms that pay a living wage. It is a popular label among small-scale chocolate producers, and one you will see often when buying high-quality chocolate.

Child Labor in Cacao Production

Of all of the issues surrounding chocolate production, the use of child labor is the most sensitive and one that many people would rather not discuss. The problem is that a majority of the cacao grown in the world comes from West Africa, where the use of child labor is widespread.

In 2001, after a BBC documentary exposed child labor in West Africa, Senator Tom Harkin and U.S. Representative Eliot Engel created the Harkin-Engel Protocol with the goal of ending the worst forms of child labor and adult forced labor on cacao farms in West Africa. The heads of eight major chocolate companies, the ambassador of the Ivory Coast, and the director of the International Program on the Elimination of Child Labor signed on.

This sounds great, but it was a compromised deal. Originally, Engel wanted a "child-labor free" label that could be enforced and verified, but the international cocoa industry strongly opposed it. The protocol was a settled deal and has no enforcement mechanism, and many believe it has made no progress in ending child labor. According to the group Stop the Traffik and a CNN report on slavery, the international chocolate industry has made almost a trillion dollars since the protocol was signed but has only invested 0.0075 percent of that into ending child slavery. The director of *The Dark Side of Chocolate,* a 2010 documentary, claims the protocol is only a political document because there has been no real progress on the issue. The issue is serious enough that some food activists refuse to eat cacao products entirely.

Fortunately, you do not have to resort to such extremes because it is possible to find ethically sourced cacao free of child labor. Another organization that works on this issue is the Food Empowerment Project (FEP). FEP is a food justice nonprofit that recognizes the power of one's food choices. It has taken on the herculean task of deciphering which companies get their chocolate from West Africa, which could very likely have been produced using child slavery. In 2010, even FLO had to suspend suppliers they were working with because child slavery was found on one of their farms. Accordingly, no current label on chocolate can guarantee that child labor is not used. FEP keeps an online list at FoodisPower.org with the following groupings, based on where and how the cacao is sourced:

- Chocolate we feel comfortable recommending
- Recommended—Giving them the benefit of the doubt
- Cannot recommend but are working on the issues in various ways
- Cannot recommend but at least responded
- Cannot recommend: companies that would not disclose their supplier (no transparency for customers)
- Cannot recommend: companies that did not respond

FEP believes that consumer pressure on companies that use cacao from farms where child labor has been found will lead to change in how the industry operates. Many people are concerned about where their cacao comes from and are willing to put in more time, work, and expense to get a better, more just product. Although there is currently no label for such, familiarizing yourself with the list and contacting companies to let them know how you feel is a great start.

Direct trade and single estate chocolate. The goal of these labels, and the certifications and organizations behind them, is to make the supply chain of cacao as transparent as possible. As conscientious consumers, I believe we have the right to know who grew our food and where it came from. The more that we know, the better it is for our health and the health of everyone involved.

One way to know more about where our cacao is coming from is single estate or direct trade chocolate. Single estate is what it sounds like: Chocolate that is created with cacao beans from one specific farm or plantation. Like coffee beans, cacao from different areas of the world has distinct tastes, and chocolate connoisseurs have specific taste preferences to regions. Some small-scale chocolate producers work directly with cacao farmers and cooperatives to produce these very specific and unique chocolate bars. Want a Belizean bar, or are you more in the mood for an Ecuadorian?

Direct trade also comes from coffee production ideals. The idea behind the movement "third wave coffee" is that coffee is artisanal like wine and not just a commodity, which led to the creation of direct trade. Working directly with each farm and not a supplier allows producers to monitor the farm themselves (they often visit to see it) and pay premiums above market rates. The Big Three of third wave coffee—Intelligentsia, Stumptown, and Counter Culture Coffee—and how these companies have transformed coffee, both in taste and equitable trade, is hopefully predictive of the artisanal value and ethics of cacao and chocolate that is to come. In my opinion, both single estate taste preferences and direct trade transparency are the future of good chocolate.

Chapter 1

Craig, W.J., Mangels, A.R., and the American Dietetic Association*. "Position of the American Dietetic Association: Vegetarian Diets," *Journal of the American Dietetic Association.* 2009 Jul;109(7):1266-82. *Now the Academy of Nutrition and Dietetics.

Doucé, L., Poels, K., Janssens, W., et al. "Smelling the books: The effect of chocolate scent on purchase-related behavior in a bookstore," *Journal of Environmental Psychology.* 2013 Dec;36(1):65-69.

Hooper, L., Kroon, P.A., Rimm, E.B., et al. "Flavonoids, Flavonoid-rich foods, and cardiovascular risk: A meta-analysis of randomized controlled trials," *American Journal of Clinical Nutrition.* 2008 Jul;88(1):38-50.

Oude Griep, L.M., Verschuren, W.M., Kromhout, D., et al. "Colours of fruit and vegetables and 10-year incidence of CHD [coronary heart disease],"*British Journal of Nutrition.* 2011 Nov;106(10):1562-9.

Williams, S., Tamburic, S., Lally, C. "Eating chocolate can significantly protect the skin from UV light," *Journal of Cosmetic Dermatology.* 2009;8:169-73.

Chapter 2

Aune, D., Chan D.S., et al. "Dietary fibre, whole grains, and risk of colorectal cancer: Systematic review and dose-response meta-analysis of prospective studies," *BMJ.* 2011 Nov 10;343:d6617.

Benzie, I.F., Wachtel-Galor, S. "Vegetarian diets and public health: Biomarker and redox connections," *Antioxidants & Redox Signaling.* 2010 Nov 15;13(10):1575-91.

Ellam, S., Williamson, G. "Cocoa and human health," *Annual Review of Nutrition.* 2013 Jul 17;33:105-28.

Habauzit, V., Morand, C. "Evidence for a protective effect of polyphenols-containing foods on cardiovascular health: an update for clinicians," *Therapeutic Advances in Chronic Disease.* 2012 Mar;3(2):87-106.

Hunter, J.E., Zhang, J., Kris-Etherton, P.M. "Cardiovascular disease risk of dietary stearic acid compared with trans, other saturated, and unsaturated fatty acids: a systematic review," *American Journal of Clinical Nutrition.* 2010 Jan;91(1):46-63.

Katz, D.L., Doughty, K., Ali, A. "Cocoa and chocolate in human health and disease," *Antioxidants & Redox Signaling.* 2011 Nov 15;15(10):2779-811.

Lawrence, G.D. "Dietary Fats and Health: Dietary recommendations in the context of scientific evidence," *Advances in Nutrition.* 2013 May 1;4(3):294-302.

Mudgil, D., Barak, S. "Composition, properties and health benefits of indigestiblecarbohydrate polymers as dietary fiber: A review," *International Journal of Biological Macromolecules.* 2013 Jul 2;61C:1-6.

Office of Dietary Supplements, National Institutes of Health. *Dietary Supplement Fact Sheet: Magnesium.* http://ods.od.nih.gov/factsheets/Magnesium-HealthProfessional/. Viewed July 30, 2013.

Schwingshackl, L., Strasser, B., Hoffmann, G. "Effects of monounsaturated fatty acids on cardiovascular risk factors: a systematic review and meta-analysis," *Annals of Nutrition and Metabolism.* 2011;59(2-4):176-86.

Simopoulos, A.P. "The importance of the omega-6/omega-3 fatty acid ratio in cardiovascular disease and other chronic diseases," *Experimental Biology and Medicine* (Maywood, N.J.). 2008 Jun;233(6):674-88.

Siri-Tarino, P.W., Sun, Q, Hu, F., et al. "Saturated fatty acids and risk of coronary heart disease: Modulation by replacement nutrients," *Current Atherosclerosis Reports.* 2010 Nov;12(6):384-90.

Wilson, N., Nghiem, N. "Foods and dietary patterns that are healthy, low-cost, and environmentally sustainable: A case study of optimization modeling for New Zealand," *PLoS One.* 2013;8(3):e59648.

Chapter 3

Atkinson, G., Batterham, A.M. "Allometric scaling of diameter change in the original flow-mediated dilation protocol," *Atherosclerosis.* 2013 Feb;226(2):425-7.

Baba, S., Natsume, M., Yasuda, A., et al. "Plasma LDL and HDL cholesterol and oxidized LDL concentrations are altered in normo- and hypercholesterolemic humans after intake of different levels of cocoa powder," *Journal of Nutrition.* 2007 Jun;137(6):1436-41.

Hertog, M.G., Kromhout, D., Aravanis, C., et al. "Flavonoid intake and long-term risk of coronary heart disease and cancer in the seven countries study," *Archives of Internal Medicine*. 1995 Feb 27;155(4):381-6.

Hooper, L., Kroon P.A., Rimm, E.B., et al. "Flavonoids, flavonoid-rich foods, and cardiovascular risk: A meta-analysis of randomized controlled trials," *American Journal of Clinical Nutrition*. 2008 Jul;88(1):38-50.

Katz, D.L., Doughty K., Ali, A. "Cocoa and chocolate in human health and disease," *Antioxidants & Redox Signaling*. 2011 Nov 15;15(10):2779-811.

Mensink, R.P. "Effects of stearic acid on plasma lipid and lipoproteins in humans," *Lipids*. 2005 Dec;40(12):1201-5.

Chapter 4

Babu, P.V., Liu, D., Gilbert, E.R. "Recent advances in understanding the anti-diabetic actions of dietary flavonoids," *Journal of Nutritional Biochemistry*. 2013 Sep 9. S0955-2863(13)00127-7 [Epub ahead of print].

Balzer, J., Rassaf, T., et al. "Sustained benefits in vascular function through flavanol- containing cocoa in medicated diabetic patients a double-masked, randomized, controlled trial," *Journal of the American College of Cardiology*. 2008 Jun 3; 51(22):2141-9.

Barnard, N.D., Katcher, H.I., et al. "Vegetarian and vegan diets in type 2 diabetes management," *Nutrition Reviews*. 2009 May;67(5):255-63.

Champagne, C.M. "Magnesium in hypertension, cardiovascular disease, metabolic syndrome, and other conditions: a review," *Nutrition and Clinical Practice*. 2008 Apr-May;23(2):142-51.

Golomb, B.A., Koperski, S., White, H.L. "Association between more frequent chocolate consumption and lower body mass index," *Archives of Internal Medicine*. 2012 Mar 26;172(6):519-21.

Greenberg, J.A., Buijsse, B. "Habitual chocolate consumption may increase body weight in a dose-response manner," *PLoS One*. 2013 Aug 7;8(8):e70271. eCollection 2013.

Hadi, H.A., Suwaidi, J.A. "Endothelial dysfunction in diabetes mellitus," *Journal of Vascular Health and Risk Management*. 2007 December; 3(6):853-76.

He, K., Liu, K., et al. "Magnesium intake and incidence of metabolic syndrome among young adults," *Circulation*. 2006 Apr 4;113(13):1675-82.

Hollenberg, N.K., Martinez, G., et al. "Aging, acculturation, salt intake, and hypertension in the Kuna of Panama," *Hypertension*. 1997 Jan;29(1 Pt 2):171-6.

Hollenberg, N.K., Fisher, N.D. "Is it the dark in dark chocolate?" *Circulation*. 2007; 116: 2360-62.

Jalil, A.M.M., Ismail, A. "Polyphenols in cocoa and cocoa products: Is there a link between antioxidant properties and health?" *Molecules* 2008, 13, 2190-219.

Kahleova, H., Matoulek, M., et al. "Vegetarian diet improves insulin resistance and oxidative stress markers more than conventional diet in subjects with Type 2 diabetes," *Diabetic Medicine*. 2011 May;28(5):549-59.

Ma, B., Lawson, A.B., et al. "Dairy, magnesium, and calcium intake in relation to insulin sensitivity: Approaches to modeling a dose-dependent association," *American Journal of Epidemiology*. 2006 Sep 1;164(5):449-58.

McCullough, M.L., Chevaux, K., et al. "Hypertension, the Kuna, and the epidemiology of flavanols," *Journal of Cardiovascular Pharmacology*. 2006;47 Suppl 2:S103-9; discussion 119-21.

Nogueira, Lde P., Knibel, M.P., et al. "Consumption of high-polyphenol dark chocolate improves endothelial function in individuals with stage 1 hypertension and excess body weight," *International Journal of Hypertension*. 2012;2012:147321.

Ried, K., Sullivan, T.R., et al. "Effect of cocoa on blood pressure," Cochrane Database of Systematic Reviews. 2012 Aug 15;8:CD008893.

Schulze, M.B., et al. "Fiber and magnesium intake and incidence of type 2 diabetes: a prospective study and meta-analysis," *Archives of Internal Medicine*. 2007, 167, 956-65.

Zomer, E., Owen, A., et al. "The effectiveness and cost effectiveness of dark chocolate consumption as prevention therapy in people at high risk of cardiovascular disease: best case scenario analysis using a Markov model," *BMJ*. 2012; 344: e3657.

Chapter 5

Andújar, I., Recio, M.C., et al. "Cocoa polyphenols and their potential benefits for human health," *Oxidative Medicine and Cellular Longevity*. 2012;2012:906252.

Camfield, D.A., Scholey, A., et al. "Steady state visually evoked potential (SSVEP) topography changes associated with cocoa flavanol consumption," *Physiology & Behavior*. 2012 Feb 28;105(4):948-57.

de la Monte, S.M., Wands, J.R. "Alzheimer's disease is type 3 diabetes–evidence reviewed," *Journal of Diabetes Science and Technology*. 2008 November; 2(6):1101–113.

EFSA. "Scientific opinion on the substantiation of a health claim related to cocoa flavanols and maintenance of normal endothelium-dependent vasodilation pursuant to Article 13(5) of Regulation (EC) No 1924/2006," *European Food Safety Authority Journal*. 2012;10(7):2809-30.

Ellam, S., Williamson, G. "Cocoa and human health," *Annual Review of Nutrition*. 2013 Jul 17;33:105-28.

Ferrières, J. "The French paradox: lessons for other countries," *Heart*. 2004;90:107-11.

Field, D.T., Williams, C.M., Butler L.T. "Consumption of cocoa flavanols results in an acute improvement in visual and cognitive functions," *Physiology & Behavior*. 2011 Jun 1;103(3-4):255-60.

Helmut, S., Tankred, S., et al. "Cocoa polyphenols and inflammatory mediators," *American Journal of Clinical Nutrition*. 2005 Jan;81(1):304S-12S.

Larsson, S.C., Virtamo, J., Wolk, A. "Chocolate consumption and risk of stroke: A prospective cohort of men and meta-analysis," *Neurology*. 2012 Sep 18; 79(12):1223-9.

Lippi, D. "Chocolate in history: Food, medicine, medi-food," *Nutrients*. 2013 May; 5(5): 1573–84.

Martin, F.P., Rezzi, S., et al. "Metabolic effects of dark chocolate consumption on energy, gut microbiota, and stress-related metabolism in free-living subjects," *Journal of Proteome Research*. 2009 Dec;8(12):5568-79.

Scholey, A.B., French, S.J., et al. "Consumption of cocoa flavanols results in acute improvements in mood and cognitive performance during sustained mental effort," *Journal of Psychopharmacology*. 2010 Oct;24(10):1505-14.

Smeets, P.A., de Graaf, C., et al. "Effect of satiety on brain activation during chocolate tasting in men and women," *American Journal of Clinical Nutrition*. 2006 Jun;83(6):1297-305.

Smit, H.J., Blackburn, R.J. "Reinforcing effects of caffeine and theobromine as found in chocolate," *Psychopharmacology*. 2005 Aug;181(1):101-6.

Smit, H.J., Gaffan, E.A., Rogers, P.J. "Methylxanthines are the psycho-pharmacologically active constituents of chocolate," *Psychopharmacology*. 2004 Nov;176(3-4):412-9.

Smit, H.J., Rogers, P.J. "Effects of low doses of caffeine on cognitive performance, mood, and thirst in low and higher caffeine consumers," *Psychopharmacology*. 2000 Oct;152(2):167-73.

Sokolov, A.N., Pavlova, M.A., et al. "Chocolate and the brain: Neurobiological impact of cocoa flavanols on cognition and behavior," *Neuroscience & Biobehavioral Reviews*. 2013 Jun 26. pii: S0149-7634(13)00168-1.

Sorond, F.A., Hurwitz, S., et al. "Neurovascular coupling, cerebral white matter integrity, and response to cocoa in older people," *Neurology*. 2013 Sep 3;81(10):904-9.

Sorond, F.A., Lipsitz, L.A., et al. "Cerebral blood flow response to flavanol-rich cocoa in healthy elderly humans," *Journal of Neuropsychiatric Disease and Treatment*. 2008 Apr;4(2):433-40.

Chapter 6

Allgrove, J., Farrell, E., et al. "Regular dark chocolate consumption's reduction of oxidative stress and increase of free-fatty-acid mobilization in response to prolonged cycling," *International Journal of Sport Nutrition and Exercise Metabolism*. 2011 Apr;21(2):113-23.

Beard, J., Tobin, B. "Iron status and exercise," *American Journal of Clinical Nutrition*. 2000 Aug;72(2 Suppl):594S-7S.

Clarkson, P.M. "Antioxidants and physical performance," *Critical Reviews in Food Science and Nutrition*. 1995 Jan;35(1-2):131-41.

Clarkson, P.M., Thompson, H.S. "Antioxidants: What role do they play in physical activity and health?" *American Journal of Clinical Nutrition.* 2000 Aug;72(2 Suppl):637S-46S.

Davis, J.K., Green, J.M. "Caffeine and anaerobic performance: ergogenic value and mechanisms of action," *Sports Medicine.* 2009;39(10):813-32.

Davison, G., Callister, R., et al. "The effect of acute pre-exercise dark chocolate consumption on plasma antioxidant status, oxidative stress and immunoendocrine responses to prolonged exercise," *European Journal of Nutrition.* 2012 Feb;51(1):69-79.

Dekkers, J.C., van Doornen, L.J., et al. "The role of antioxidant vitamins and enzymes in the prevention of exercise-induced muscle damage," *Sports Medicine.* 1996 Mar;21(3):213-38.

Finaud, J., Lac, G., Filaire, E. "Oxidative stress: Relationship with exercise and training," *Sports Medicine.* 2006;36(4):327-58.

Fisher, N.D., Hughes, M., et al. "Flavanol-rich cocoa induces nitric-oxide-dependent vasodilation in healthy humans," *Journal of Hypertension.* 2003 Dec;21(12):2281-6.

Fisher, N.D., Hurwitz, S., et al. "Habitual flavonoid intake and endothelial function in healthy humans," *Journal of the American College of Nutrition.* 2012 Aug;31(4):275-9.

Hillary, E. *High Adventure: The True Story of the First Ascent of Everest.* Oxford University Press; 2003.

Lansley, K.E., Winyard, P.G., et al. "Acute dietary nitrate supplementation improves cycling time trial performance," *Medicine & Science in Sports & Exercise* 2011 Jun;43(6):1125-31.

Lukaski, H.C., Nielsen, F.H.J. "Dietary magnesium depletion affects metabolic responses during submaximal exercise in postmenopausal women," *Journal of Nutrition.* 2002 May; 132(5):930-5.

Malaguti, M., Angeloni, C., et al. "Polyphenols in exercise performance and prevention of exercise-induced muscle damage," *Oxidative Medicine and Cellular Longevity* 2013; 2013:825928.

Powers, S.K., Jackson, M.J. "Exercise-induced oxidative stress: cellular mechanisms and impact on muscle force production," *Physiological Reviews* 2008 Oct;88(4):1243-76.

Santos, D.A., Matias, C.N., et al. "Magnesium intake is associated with strength performance in elite basketball, handball and volleyball players," *Magnesium Research* 2011 Dec;24(4):215-9.

Smit, H.J. "Theobromine and the pharmacology of cocoa," *Handbook of Experimental Pharmacology* 2011;(200):201-34.

Trapp, D., Knez, W., Sinclair, W. "Could a vegetarian diet reduce exercise-induced oxidative stress? A review of the literature," *Journal of Sports Sciences.* 2010 Oct;28(12):1261-8.

Weinberg, B.A., Bealer, B.K. *The World of Caffeine.* Routledge; 2002.

Woolf, K., Bidwell, W.K., et al. "The effect of caffeine as an ergogenic aid in anaerobic exercise," *International Journal of Sport Nutrition and Exercise Metabolism.* 2008 Aug;18(4):412-29.

Appendix

Accardi, G., Caruso, C., et al. "Can Alzheimer disease be a form of type 3 diabetes?" *Rejuvenation Research.* 2012 Apr;15(2):217-21.

Miller, K.B., Hurst, W.J., et al. "Impact of alkalization on the antioxidant and flavanol content of commercial cocoa powders," *Journal of Agricultural and Food Chemistry.* 2008 Sep 24;56(18):8527-33.

About the Authors & Acknowledgments

Matthew Ruscigno, M.P.H., R.D., is a registered dietitian and has nutrition degrees from Pennsylvania State University and Loma Linda University. He is the past chair of the Vegetarian Nutrition Practice Group of the Academy of Nutrition and Dietetics as well as the co-author of *No Meat Athlete* (Fair Winds Press, 2013) with Matt Frazier and *Appetite For Reduction* with Isa Moskowitz. In addition to his private practice and public speaking, Matt is a recreational athlete who has completed in ultra-marathons, iron-distance triathlons, 24-hour mountain bike races, and the Furnace Creek 508, a nonstop 500-mile bike race through Death Valley. He writes about fun, adventure, and nutrition at www.truelovehealth.com.

Joshua Ploeg has been a vegan personal chef/caterer, writer, and punk musician since the 1990s. He has spent the last ten years touring the United States and the world, cooking in varied and interesting circumstances from place to place. He has penned several cookbooks, including *This Ain't No Picnic*, *In Search of the Lost Taste*, and *Something Delicious This Way Comes: Spellbinding Vegan Cookery*. He has also contributed recipes and columns to various publications including Brooklyn's *Satya* magazine.

Every big project arises from the work of many people, and this is no exception. The first thank you goes to my co-author Joshua Ploeg for his creative genius and willingness to do this book. It would not have happened without his exceptional culinary skills. Also, Cara Connors and the staff at Quarto were immensely helpful. Carolyn Tampe, R.D., served as a valuable research assistant, and Lauren Ornelas from the Food Empowerment Project took time from her own work to answer my onslaught of questions about cacao production. Robbie Stout from Ritual Chocolate gave me a tour of their "chocolate factory" and was happy to explain the intricacies of chocolate making to me more than once. My registered dietitian colleagues provide immeasurable support in everything I do.

There are too many to name, but a lot of them I know through the Vegetarian Nutrition Dietary Practice Group of the Academy of Nutrition and Dietetics. Thank you for all you do. Additionally, this book would not be possible without all of the scientists who work with cacao, chocolate, or any of the specific components. It was a pleasure to read all of your research, and I hope to have done it justice. Jaime Kulick has been reading over my work since middle school, and she was kind enough to provide feedback for this, too; Thank you. My mother, the first chocolate lover I knew, and my immediate family are always supportive and I appreciate them immensely. Caroline Netschert gave me valuable recipe feedback, and many friends simply dealt with me while I obsessed over cacao. Thank you all for being in my life!